Augmented Marked Graphs

King Sing Cheung

Augmented Marked Graphs

Springer

King Sing Cheung
Director of Information Technology
The Open University of Hong Kong
Hong Kong
Hong Kong SAR

ISBN 978-3-319-35760-7   ISBN 978-3-319-06428-4 (eBook)
DOI 10.1007/978-3-319-06428-4
Springer Cham Heidelberg New York Dordrecht London

Printed on acid-free paper

Springer is part of Springer Science+Business Media (www.springer.com)

To my parents in memory.

Preface

Petri nets are a formal and theoretically rich model for the modelling and analysis of systems. A subclass of Petri nets, augmented marked graphs possess a structure that is especially desirable for the modelling and analysis of systems with concurrent processes and shared resources.

Augmented marked graphs are rather new in the literature, as compared to other subclasses of Petri nets. They were extensively studied in the past decade. I am one among a few researchers who have continuously studied augmented marked graphs since their inception. In 2012, I began to review and consolidate my research papers on augmented marked graphs and organize them as a research monograph which covers both the theoretical and application aspects of augmented marked graphs. This book is therefore written to provide a comprehensive description of augmented marked graphs, with every notion explained and every theoretical result proved. Clear exposition is given to the special properties of augmented marked graphs and the property-preserving composition of augmented marked graphs. The application to system integration for component-based systems and manufacturing systems are illustrated.

There are three parts in this book. Part I provides the conceptual background for readers who have no prior knowledge on Petri nets. Part II elaborates the theory of augmented marked graphs. The composition of augmented marked graphs is also investigated. Part III discusses the application to system integration for component-based systems and manufacturing systems. In this book, a number of assumptions have been made. First, the terms Petri nets and place-transition nets are used interchangeably. Second, unless specified otherwise, all place-transition nets are pure and ordinary place-transition nets. Third, a place-transition net contains no disjoint subnets. Fourth, there are no source places, source transitions, sink places, or sink transitions in a place-transition net. Fifth, for a place-transition net, all paths are regarded as elementary paths, and all cycles as elementary cycles, unless specified otherwise.

This book is the first self-contained volume on augmented marked graphs in the literature. It is useful to both researchers and practitioners in the fields of Petri nets and system integration.

Hong Kong, Hong Kong SAR   King Sing Cheung

Acknowledgements

I would like to express my thanks to To Yat Cheung who was my PhD supervisor. He enlightened me on the theory of Petri nets. His insightful advice inspired me in developing the theory of augmented marked graphs.

I am grateful to many anonymous researchers who helped review my earlier works on augmented marked graphs, which were published as journal articles, book chapters, and conference papers. Their constructive comments were useful for me to improve my research on augmented marked graphs.

I am also grateful to Ronan Nugent who rendered assistance to me in publishing this book in Springer's Computer Science series.

Last but not least, I would like to thank my wife Wing Ki and my children Ho Ching and Ho Hei for their endless encouragement and support.

Hong Kong, Hong Kong SAR   King Sing Cheung
February 2014

Contents

List of Symbols

Sets, Sequences, and Logic Operators

$\{\ldots\}$	A set
$\langle\ldots\rangle$	A sequence
$(\ldots)$	A vector
$\cup$	Union
$\cap$	Intersection
$\setminus$	Difference
$\subseteq$ ($\not\subseteq$)	A subset of (not a subset of)
$\subset$ ($\not\subset$)	A proper subset of (not a proper subset of)
$\in$ ($\notin$)	An element of (not an element of)
$\varnothing$	Empty set or null
$\forall$	Universal quantifier
$\exists$	Existential quantifier
$\times$	Cartesian product
$\lvert X \rvert$	The cardinality of X
X^+	Kleene closure of X
$\wedge$	And
$\vee$	Or
$\Rightarrow$	Logical implication

Petri Nets

p_i	A place
t_i	A transition
σ	A firing sequence
ρ	A path

α	A place vector or place invariant
β	A transition vector or transition invariant
μ	A firing vector
V	An incident matrix
M	A marking
(N, M_0)	A PT-net N with an initial marking M_0
$M[N,t\rangle$	Transition t being enabled at M in N
$M[N,t\rangle M'$	M' being reachable from M after firing transition t in N
$M[N,\sigma\rangle$	Firing sequence σ being enabled at M in N
$M[N,\sigma\rangle M'$	M' being reachable from M after firing sequence σ in N
$M[N,*\rangle M'$	M' being reachable from M in N
$[N,M_0\rangle$	The set of reachable markings of N
γ	A cycle
Y	A set of cycles
Ω_N	The set of cycles in a PT-net N
$\Omega_N[p]$	The set of cycles in N, each of which contains place p
P[Y]	The set of places contained in a set of cycles Y
T[Y]	The set of transitions generated by a set of cycles Y

Augmented Marked Graphs

$(N, M_0; R)$	An augmented marked graph
R	The set of resource places
r	A resource place
D_r	The set of transition pairs for a resource place r
R-siphon	A siphon containing at least a resource place
NR-siphon	A siphon not containing any resource place
R_F	The set of fused resource places in the integrated augmented marked graph
R_F-siphon	A siphon containing at least a place in R_F in the integrated augmented marked graph

Part I
Basic Concepts

Chapter 1
Introduction

This chapter aims to provide some background for the readers to understand the motivation of using augmented marked graphs in the modelling and analysis of systems. It starts with some basic concepts of system design. The challenges in system integration are discussed. It then introduces augmented marked graphs, and discusses how they can be effectively used in modelling and analyzing systems to address the challenges in system integration. An overview of the subsequent chapters of this book is also provided.

1.1 Fundamentals of System Design

A system is literally defined as an integrated whole of interacting, inter-related or inter-dependent components, modules or objects that accomplish some functional purposes [1–3]. In general, a system can be viewed from two different perspectives, structure and behaviour. A system possesses a static structure, showing how its components, modules or objects are structurally organized, inter-related or inter-depended. On the other hand, a system exhibits a collection of behavioural patterns, each delineating how the inter-related or inter-dependent components, modules or objects interact for some functional purposes.

Nowadays, computer systems and automated systems are usually large and complex. Structuring a system into manageable components or modules is deemed an effective means to manage complexity and enable reuse of components or modules. This approach to designing and implementing a system is called component-based system design [4–7]. In the past two decades, component-based system design has emerged as a promising system design methodology. It emphasizes the compositional synthesis of a system from its components or modules, and the maximal reuse of components or modules.

Typically, the system design process begins with collecting the functional requirements from users. These requirements are usually described as the cases of how a system can be used, or use cases. Based on the requirements given as use

K.S. Cheung, *Augmented Marked Graphs*, DOI 10.1007/978-3-319-06428-4_1,
© Springer International Publishing Switzerland 2014

cases, the system designer defines the structure and behaviour of the components or modules of the system. A system is then synthesized from these components or modules. This essential step is called system integration.

It is important in system design that the correctness of the integrated system can be assured. This correctness, usually called design correctness, means that the integrated system should be free from erroneous situations such as deadlock and capacity overflow, especially for systems with distributed modules or components sharing some common resources. In system engineering terminology, it is desirable that the system is live (implying freeness from deadlock), bounded (implying freeness from capacity overflow) and reversible (capable of being re-initialized). Liveness, boundedness and reversibility collectively characterize a robust system. In system design, it is essentially required to ensure the design correctness in the sense that the integrated system is live, bounded and reversible, and, if not, identify all the possible erroneous situations.

1.2   Challenges in System Integration

In system integration, the system designer needs to meet a number of challenges in ensuring the design correctness of the integrated system. These challenges are elaborated below.

In designing component-based systems, it is difficult for the system designer to ensure that the integrated system is free from erroneous situations, such as deadlock and capacity overflow. For a system with distributed components or modules, deadlocks would occur when two or more interacting components are each waiting for the other to finish, and thus neither ever does. They are usually competing with each other for some common resources. Capacity overflow occurs when the capacity of a component exceeds its defined limit, for example, a memory chip exceeds its limit or capacity. There are other erroneous situations, for example, the system cannot be reinitialized at a particular state.

In component-based system design, a system is designed and implemented in terms of components or modules. The target system is obtained through the composition or integration of the components or modules [4–7]. In order to ensure the design correctness of the integrated system, the system designer should first ensure that every component or module of the system is free from erroneous situations. However, this does not guarantee that the integrated system can be free from erroneous situations. Deadlock may occur, especially when the components or modules are competing with others for some common resources. Capacity overflow may also occur after the system integration.

Without formal or mathematically sound techniques for modelling the components and analyzing the properties of the integrated system, it is difficult to ensure that the system integration is completely error-free. The system designer needs to walk through all possible execution scenarios of the system, and the process is very time-consuming.

1.3 Petri Nets and Augmented Marked Graphs

Modelling and analysis are two essential techniques in system design. The purpose of modelling is to represent a system and specify it in a formal and unambiguous way. Unless a system is formally and unambiguously specified, the system designer can hardly analyze the system and ensure its design correctness. It is desirable that the modelling constructs have a strong mathematical foundation to allow rigorous analysis of the system.

There are many methods and tools for modelling and analysis of systems. The Petri net is one with a strong theoretical foundation [8, 9]. Its mathematically sound modelling constructs support rigorous analysis. In graphical presentation, a Petri net is a bipartite directed graph consisting of two sorts of nodes called places and transitions, such that no arcs connect two nodes of the same sort. A place is represented by a circle, a transition by a box, and an arc by a directed line. Tokens can be assigned to places, and are represented as dots. Figure 1.1 shows an example of a Petri net. In the literature, the Petri net has been studied extensively, and a rich set of theories is available [10–13].

As a subclass of Petri nets, augmented marked graphs were first introduced by Chu for modelling systems with shared resources [14]. A thorough investigation on the properties of augmented marked graphs was reported in the literature [15–19]. Augmented marked graphs are not well known, as compared to other subclasses of Petri nets, such as state machines, marked graphs and free choice nets. However, augmented marked graphs possess a special structure which is desirable for modelling and analyzing systems with shared resources, such as manufacturing systems [14, 20, 21].

In an augmented marked graph, a set of special places is defined for representing the shared resources. These places are called resource places. If removing the resource places and their associated arcs, an augmented marked graph would become a marked graph. Figure 1.2 shows an augmented marked graph, where r_1 and r_2 are resource places. In the literature, there are two main areas of study on the theory of augmented marked graphs. The first area is on the properties of augmented marked graphs such as liveness, boundedness, reversibility, conservativeness and reachability [14–19]. The second area is on the composition of augmented marked graphs, where the focus is placed on the preservation of properties after composition [22–26].

1.4 Organization of This Book

This book provides a detailed description of augmented marked graphs, and shows how augmented marked graphs can be used in the modelling and analysis of systems. The application to system integration will be discussed and illustrated with real-life examples.

This book has three parts, structured as follows. Part I (Chaps. 1 and 2) aims to provide some conceptual background for the readers. Following this introduction,

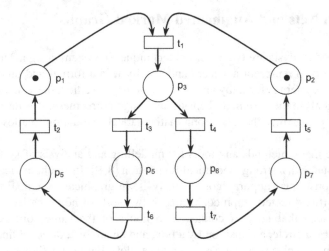

Fig. 1.1 Example of a Petri net

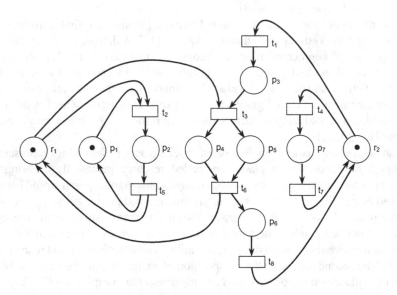

Fig. 1.2 Example of an augmented marked graph

Chap. 2 covers the fundamentals of Petri nets. It begins with introducing the definition and terminology of Petri nets. A detailed description of the properties of Petri nets then follows. This chapter also presents two well-known subclasses of Petri nets, namely, state machines and marked graphs, which will be referred in the subsequent chapters.

Part II (Chaps. 3–6) covers the theoretical aspects of augmented marked graphs. Chapter 3 states the formal definition of augmented marked graphs.

Characterizations for their liveness, boundedness, reversibility and conservativeness are elaborated. Chapter 4 introduces a special type of augmented marked graphs, called proper augmented marked graphs. The special properties of proper augmented marked graphs are discussed. Chapter 5 investigates the composition of augmented marked graphs. It shows how augmented marked graphs are composed via their common resource places to form an integrated augmented marked graph. A special focus is placed on the preservation of properties, such as liveness, reversibility, boundedness and conservativeness. Chapter 6 then shows how augmented marked graphs can be used for modelling and analyzing a system, with the Dining Philosophers problem as an example for illustration. The beauty of property-preserving composition is discussed.

Part III (Chaps. 7 and 8) covers the application aspects of augmented marked graphs. Chapter 7 describes the application to component-based system integration. It highlights the challenges in ensuring the design correctness of the integrated system, and shows how augmented marked graphs can be used for modelling components, how they are composed to form an integrated system, and how the design correctness of the system can be effectively analyzed. Chapter 8 illustrates the application to manufacturing system integration, showing how augmented marked graphs can be used for modelling manufacturing system components, how they are composed to form an integrated manufacturing system, and how the design correctness of the manufacturing system can be effectively analyzed.

Chapter 9 provides a summary, and concludes this book with a brief discussion on the direction for further studies.

References

1. Definition of "system", in *The Merriam-Webster's Collegiate Dictionary*, 11th edn. (Merriam-Webster, 2003)
2. Definition of "system", in *The Oxford Dictionary of English*, 3rd edn. (Oxford University Press, 2010)
3. C. Haskins (ed.), *INCOSE Systems Engineering Handbook: A Guide for System Life Cycle Processes and Activities* (International Council of System Engineering, San Diego, 2010)
4. G.T. Leavens, M. Sitaraman (eds.), *Foundations of Component-Based Systems* (Cambridge University Press, Cambridge, 2000)
5. G.T. Heineman, W.T. Councill, *Component-Based Software Engineering: Putting the Pieces Together* (Addison-Wesley, Boston, 2002)
6. C. Szyperski, *Component Software: Beyond Object-Oriented Programming* (Addison-Wesley, Reading, 2002)
7. M. Ramachandran, *Software Components: Guidelines and Applications* (Nova, New York, 2008)
8. C.A. Petri, *Kommunikation mit Automaten*, PhD dissertation, University of Bonn, Germany, 1962
9. C.A. Petri, *Communication with automata*, DTIC Research Report AD0630125, Defense Technical Information Centre, 1966
10. J.L. Peterson, *Petri Net Theory and the Modeling of System* (Prentice Hall, Englewood Cliffs, 1981)

11. W. Reisig, *Petri Nets: An Introduction* (Springer, Berlin, 1985)
12. T. Murata, Petri nets: properties, analysis and applications. Proc. IEEE **77**(4), 541–580 (1989)
13. J. Desel, W. Reisig, Place transition Petri nets, in *Lectures on Petri Nets I: Basic Models*, ed. by W. Reisig, G. Rozenberg. Lecture Notes in Computer Science, vol. 1491 (Springer, Berlin, 1998), pp. 122–173
14. F. Chu, X. Xie, Deadlock analysis of Petri nets using siphons and mathematical programming. IEEE Trans. Robot. Autom. **13**(5), 793–804 (1997)
15. K.S. Cheung, New characterisation for live and reversible augmented marked graphs. Inf. Process. Lett. **92**(5), 239–243 (2004)
16. K.S. Cheung, K.O. Chow, Cycle-inclusion property of augmented marked graphs. Inf. Process. Lett. **94**(6), 271–276 (2005)
17. K.S. Cheung, Boundedness and conservativeness of augmented marked graphs. IMA J. Math. Control. Inf. **24**(2), 235–244 (2007)
18. K.S. Cheung, Augmented marked graphs. Informatica **32**(1), 85–94 (2008)
19. C.L. Chen, S.C. Chin, H.C. Yen, Reachability analysis of augmented marked graphs via integer linear programming. Comput. J. **53**(6), 623–633 (2009)
20. K.S. Cheung, Modelling and analysis of manufacturing systems using augmented marked graphs. Inf. Technol. Control **35**(1), 19–26 (2006)
21. K.S. Cheung, Augmented marked graphs and the analysis of shared resource systems, in *Petri Net: Theory and Application*, ed. by V. Kordic (I-Tech Publishing, Vienna, 2008), pp. 377–400
22. K.S. Cheung, A formal method for synthesising components of shared resource systems. Int. J. Comput. Syst. Sci. Eng. **22**(6), 349–358 (2007)
23. K.S. Cheung, K.O. Chow, Compositional synthesis of augmented marked graphs, in *Proceedings of the IEEE International Conference on Control and Automation* (IEEE Press, 2007), pp. 2810–2814
24. K.S. Cheung, Composition of augmented marked graphs and its application to component-based system design. Inf. Technol. Control **36**(3), 310–317 (2007)
25. K.S. Cheung, Compositional synthesis of distributed system components based on augmented marked graphs. J. Comput. Sci. Technol. **8**(1), 34–40 (2008)
26. H.J. Huang, L. Jiao, T.Y. Cheung, Property-preserving composition of augmented marked graphs that share common resources, in *Proceedings of the International Conference on Robotics and Automation* (IEEE Press, 2003)

Chapter 2
Petri Nets

This chapter provides the fundamentals of Petri nets to be used in this book, especially for readers who have no prior knowledge of Petri nets. It starts with the basic definition and terminology of Petri nets. These are followed by a comprehensive description of the properties of Petri nets, such as liveness, boundedness, reversibility and conservativeness. Algebraic characterizations of the properties are also provided. We then discuss two well-known subclasses of Petri nets, namely, state machines and marked graphs. They will be referenced in the subsequence chapters of this book.

2.1 Definition and Terminology

Petri nets were found by Petri in his PhD dissertation in 1962 [1, 2], and, since then, have been developed into a theoretically sound tool for the modelling and analysis of systems [3–6]. Petri nets are commonly known as place-transition nets or PT-nets.

A PT-net is basically a bipartite directed graph consisting of two sorts of nodes called places and transitions, such that no arcs connect two nodes of the same sort. In graphical notation, a place is represented by a circle, a transition by a thick bar or a rectangular box, and an arc by a directed line. Formally, a PT-net is defined as a 4-tuple, as follows.

Definition 2.1 A place-transition net (PT-net) is a 4-tuple $N = \langle P, T, F, W \rangle$, where P is a set of places, T is a set of transitions, $F \subseteq (P \times T) \cup (T \times P)$ is a flow relation that represents the arcs, and $W : F \rightarrow \{1, 2, \ldots\}$ is a weight function which assigns a weight to every arc.

Definition 2.2 A PT-net $N = \langle P, T, F, W \rangle$ is said to be pure or self-loop free if and only if $\forall x, y \in (P \cup T) : (x, y) \in F \Rightarrow (y, x) \notin F$.

K.S. Cheung, *Augmented Marked Graphs*, DOI 10.1007/978-3-319-06428-4_2,
© Springer International Publishing Switzerland 2014

Fig. 2.1 A pure, simple and
ordinary PT-net

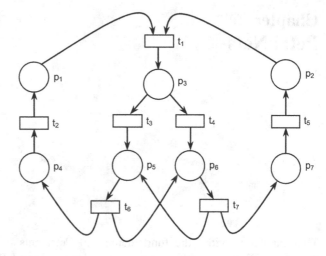

Definition 2.3 A PT-net $N = \langle P, T, F, W \rangle$ is said to be ordinary if and only if the
range of W is $\{1\}$. An ordinary PT-net can be written as $\langle P, T, F \rangle$.

Definition 2.4 Let $N = \langle P, T, F, W \rangle$ be a PT-net. For $x \in (P \cup T)$, $^{\bullet}x = \{y \mid (y, x)$
$\in F\}$ and $x^{\bullet} = \{y \mid (x, y) \in F\}$ are called the pre-set and post-set of x, respectively.

Definition 2.5 A PT-net $N = \langle P, T, F, W \rangle$ is said to be simple if and only if $\forall$ x, y
$\in (P \cup T) : (^{\bullet}x = {}^{\bullet}y \wedge x^{\bullet} = y^{\bullet}) \Rightarrow x = y$.

Throughout this book, unless specified otherwise, all PT-nets refer to pure and
ordinary PT-nets.

Example 2.1 Figure 2.1 shows an ordinary PT-net $N = \langle P, T, F, W \rangle$, where $P =$
$\{p_1, p_2, p_3, p_4, p_5, p_6, p_7\}$, $T = \{t_1, t_2, t_3, t_4, t_5, t_6, t_7\}$, $F = \{(p_1, t_1), (p_2, t_1), (t_1, p_3),$
$(t_2, p_1), (p_3, t_3), (p_3, t_4), (t_5, p_2), (p_4, t_2), (t_3, p_5), (t_4, p_6), (p_7, t_5), (t_6, p_4), (p_5, t_6), (t_6,$
$p_6), (p_6, t_7), (t_7, p_5), (t_7, p_7)\}$, and $W = F \rightarrow \{1\}$. N is self-loop free (or pure) since $\forall$
$x, y \in (P \cup T) : (x, y) \in F \Rightarrow (y, x) \notin F$.

Let us consider t_1 and p_3. The pre-set and post-set of t_1 are $^{\bullet}t_1 = \{p_1, p_2\}$ and $t_1^{\bullet} =$
$\{p_3\}$, respectively. The pre-set and post-set of p_3 are $^{\bullet}p_3 = \{t_1\}$ and $p_3^{\bullet} = \{t_3, t_4\}$,
respectively. N is also a simple PT-net since $\forall$ x, y $\in (P \cup T) : (^{\bullet}x = {}^{\bullet}y \wedge x^{\bullet} = y^{\bullet})$
$\Rightarrow x = y$.

Paths and cycles are sequences of places or transitions. They are formally
defined as follows.

Definition 2.6 For a PT-net $N = \langle P, T, F \rangle$, a path (or directed path) is a sequence
of places or transitions $\langle x_1, x_2, \ldots, x_n \rangle$, where $(x_i, x_{i+1}) \in F$ for $i = 1, 2, \ldots, n\text{-}1$. A
path is said to be elementary if and only if it does not contain the same place or
transition more than once.

Definition 2.7 For a PT-net $N = \langle P, T, F \rangle$, the notation $x (F^+) y$ means the
existence of a path in F connecting x to y.

Definition 2.8 For a PT-net $N = \langle P, T, F \rangle$, a cycle (or elementary cycle) is a sequence of places $\langle p_1, p_2, \ldots, p_n \rangle$, where there exist $t_1, t_2, \ldots, t_n \in T$ such that $\langle p_1, t_1, p_2, t_2, \ldots, p_n, t_n \rangle$ forms an elementary path and $(t_n, p_1) \in F$.

Example 2.2 Consider the PT-net $N = \langle P, T, F \rangle$ shown in Fig. 2.1. $\rho_1 = \langle p_1, t_1, p_3, t_3, p_5 \rangle$, $\rho_2 = \langle p_2, t_1, p_3, t_4, p_6, t_7, p_7, t_6 \rangle$, $\rho_3 = \langle p_3, t_3, p_5, t_6, p_4, t_2, p_1, t_1, p_3, t_4, p_6 \rangle$ and $\rho_4 = \langle p_3, t_4, p_6, t_7, p_7, t_6, p_2, t_1, p_3, t_3, p_5 \rangle$ are some paths in N. ρ_1 and ρ_2 are elementary paths since they contain no duplicate places or transitions. ρ_3 is not an elementary path since p_3 appears twice. ρ_4 is not an elementary path since p_3 appears twice.

$\gamma_1 = \langle p_1, p_3, p_5, p_4 \rangle$ is a cycle (or elementary cycle) since there exist $t_1, t_2, t_3, t_6 \in T$ such that $\langle p_1, t_1, p_3, t_3, p_5, t_6, p_4, t_2 \rangle$ forms an elementary path and $(t_2, p_1) \in F$. $\gamma_2 = \langle p_2, p_3, p_6, p_7 \rangle$ is another cycle since there exist $t_1, t_4, t_7, t_5 \in T$ such that $\langle p_2, t_1, p_3, t_4, p_6, t_7, p_7, t_5 \rangle$ forms an elementary path and $(t_5, p_2) \in F$.

Definition 2.9 A subnet of a PT-net $N = \langle P, T, F \rangle$ is itself a PT-net $S = \langle P_S, T_S, F_S \rangle$, where $P_S \subseteq P$, $T_S \subseteq T$, $F_S = F \cap ((P_S \times T_S) \cup (T_S \times P_S))$.

Definition 2.10 Two subnets $S_1 = \langle P_1, T_1, F_1 \rangle$ and $S_2 = \langle P_2, T_2, F_2 \rangle$ of a PT-net are said to be disjoint if and only if $P_1 \cap P_2 = \varnothing$ and $T_1 \cap T_2 = \varnothing$.

Definition 2.11 A PT-net $N = \langle P, T, F \rangle$ is said to be connected if and only if there does not exist two disjoint subnets $S_1 = \langle P_1, T_1, F_1 \rangle$ and $S_2 = \langle P_2, T_2, F_2 \rangle$ of N such that $P = P_1 \cup P_2$, $T = T_1 \cup T_2$ and $F = F_1 \cup F_2$.

Definition 2.12 A PT-net $N = \langle P, T, F \rangle$ is said to be strongly connected if and only if $\forall x, y \in (P \cup T) : x \ (F^+) \ y$.

Example 2.3 Figure 2.2 shows a PT-net $N = \langle P, T, F \rangle$, where $P = \{p_1, p_2, p_3, p_4, p_5, p_6, p_7, p_8, p_9, p_{10}\}$, $T = \{t_1, t_2, t_3, t_4, t_5, t_6, t_7, t_8, t_9, t_{10}\}$, $F = \{(p_1, t_1), (p_2, t_1), (t_1, p_3), (t_1, p_1), (p_3, t_3), (p_3, t_4), (t_5, p_2), (p_4, t_2), (p_5, t_2), (t_3, p_6), (t_4, p_6), (t_5, p_7), (t_6, p_4), (t_6, p_5), (p_6, t_7), (t_8, p_7), (t_9, p_7), (t_6, p_8), (t_7, p_9), (p_{10}, t_8), (p_{10}, t_9), (t_{10}, p_8), (t_{10}, p_{10})\}$.

S_1 and S_2 are subnets of N. $S_1 = \langle P_1, T_1, F_1 \rangle$ is a PT-net, where $P_1 = \{p_1, p_4, p_5, p_8\} \subseteq P$, $T_1 = \{t_2, t_6\} \subseteq T$, $F_1 = \{(t_2, p_1), (p_4, t_2), (p_5, t_2), (t_6, p_4), (t_6, p_5), (p_8, t_6)\} = F \cap ((P_1 \times T_1) \cup (T_1 \times P_1))$. Similarly, $S_2 = \langle P_2, T_2, F_2 \rangle$ is also a PT-net, where $P_2 = \{p_2, p_7, p_{10}\} \subseteq P$, $T_2 = \{t_5, t_8, t_9\} \subseteq T$, $F_2 = \{(t_5, p_2), (p_7, t_5), (t_8, p_7), (t_9, p_7), (p_{10}, t_8), (p_{10}, t_9)\} = F \cap ((P_2 \times T_2) \cup (T_2 \times P_2))$. S_1 and S_2 are disjoint subnets since $P_1 \cap P_2 = \varnothing$ and $T_1 \cap T_2 = \varnothing$.

Example 2.4 The PT-net $N = \langle P, T, F \rangle$ shown in Fig. 2.1 is connected since N does not contain any two disjoint subnets $S_1 = \langle P_1, T_1, F_1 \rangle$ and $S_2 = \langle P_2, T_2, F_2 \rangle$ such that $P = P_1 \cup P_2$, $T = T_1 \cup T_2$ and $F = F_1 \cup F_2$. N is also a strongly connected PT-net since $\forall x, y \in (P \cup T) : x \ (F^+) \ y$.

Example 2.5 Figure 2.3 shows another PT-net $N = \langle P, T, F \rangle$, which is connected since N does not contain any two disjoint subnets $S_1 = \langle P_1, T_1, F_1 \rangle$ and $S_2 = \langle P_2, T_2, F_2 \rangle$ such that $P = P_1 \cup P_2$, $T = T_1 \cup T_2$ and $F = F_1 \cup F_2$. N is not a strongly connected PT-net because the condition $\forall x, y \in (P \cup T) : x \ (F^+) \ y$ does not hold.

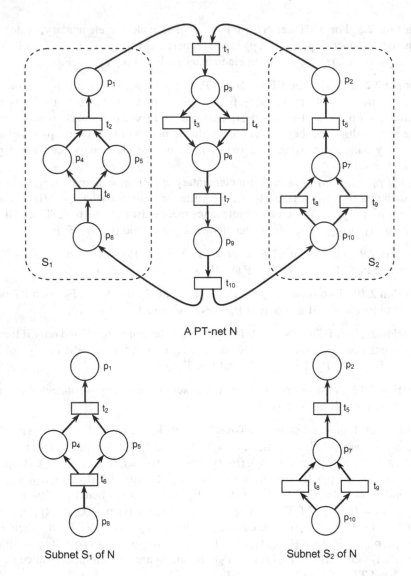

Fig. 2.2 A PT-net N, and two subnets S_1 and S_2 of N

For example, there does not exist any path connecting p_2 to p_7, nor any path connecting p_4 to p_6.

For a PT-net, a marking denotes the assignment of tokens to its places. In graphical notation, a token is represented by a black dot. A marking is formally defined as follows.

Definition 2.13 Let $N = \langle P, T, F \rangle$ be a PT-net, where $P = \{p_1, p_2, \ldots, p_n\}$. N is said to be marked if some tokens are assigned to its places. A marking is defined as a

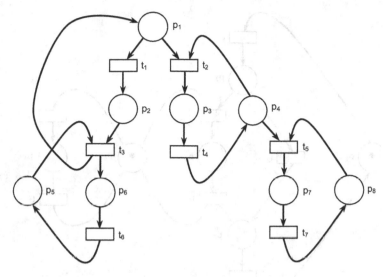

Fig. 2.3 A PT-net which is connected but not strongly connected

function $M : P \rightarrow \{0, 1, 2, \ldots\}$, where $M(p)$ represents the number of tokens assigned to a place $p \in P$. Alternatively, M can be expressed as a place vector $(M(p_1), M(p_2), \ldots, M(p_n))$. (N, M_0) represents N with an initial marking M_0, and can be written as $\langle P, T, F, M_0 \rangle$.

Example 2.6 Figure 2.4 shows a PT-net (N, M_0), where $N = \langle P, T, F \rangle$ and M_0 is the initial marking. A token is assigned to place p_1. Another token is assigned to place p_2. The token assignment is denoted by an initial marking $M_0 : P \rightarrow \{0, 1\}$, such that $M_0(p_1) = 1$, $M_0(p_2) = 1$, $M_0(p_3) = 0$, $M_0(p_4) = 0$, $M_0(p_5) = 0$ and $M_0(p_6) = 0$. M_0 can be expressed as a place vector $(1, 1, 0, 0, 0, 0)$.

A transition is firable when every place in its pre-set holds sufficient number of tokens. On firing a transition, tokens are removed from the places in its pre-set and assigned to the places in its post-set. The firability of transitions is formally defined as follows.

Definition 2.14 For a PT-net $N = \langle P, T, F, W \rangle$, a transition $t \in T$ is said to be firable (or enabled) at a marking M if and only if $\forall p \in {}^\bullet t : M(p) \geq W(p,t)$. After firing t, M is changed to M' such that $\forall p \in P : M'(p) = M(p) - W(p,t) + W(t,p)$, in notation, $M [N,t\rangle M'$.

Definition 2.15 For a PT-net (N, M_0), a sequence of transitions $\sigma = \langle t_1, t_2, \ldots, t_n \rangle$ is said to be firable (or enabled) at M_0 if and only if there exists a set of markings $\{M_1, M_2, \ldots, M_n\}$ such that $M_{i-1} [N,t_i\rangle M_i$, for $i = 1, 2, \ldots, n$. After firing σ, M_0 is changed to M_n, in notation, $M_0 [N,\sigma\rangle M_n$.

When there is no confusion in the context, $M [N,t\rangle M'$ and $M_0 [N,\sigma\rangle M_n$ can be written as $M [t\rangle M'$ and $M_0 [\sigma\rangle M_n$ respectively.

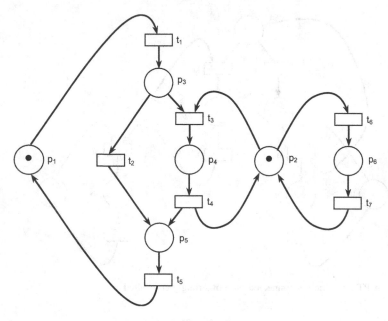

Fig. 2.4 A PT-net (N, M_0) with an initial marking M_0

Example 2.7 Consider the PT-net (N, M_0) in Fig. 2.4, where $M_0 = (1, 1, 0, 0, 0, 0)$. At the initial marking M_0, t_1 is firable. On firing t_1, M_0 is changed to a new marking $M_1 = (0, 1, 1, 0, 0, 0)$, in notation, $M_0 [N,t_1\rangle M_1$. The token in p_1 is removed, and a token is assigned to p_3. At M_1, both t_2 and t_3 are firable. On firing t_3, M_1 is changed to a new marking $M_2 = (0, 0, 0, 1, 0, 0)$, in notation, $M_1 [N,t_3\rangle M_2$. The tokens in p_2 and p_3 are removed, and a token is assigned to p_4. Then, at M_2, t_4 is firable. On firing t_4, M_2 is changed to a new marking $M_3 = (0, 1, 0, 0, 1, 0)$, in notation, $M_2 [N,t_4\rangle M_3$. Figure 2.5 shows the PT-net (N, M_3) obtained from (N, M_0) after firing $\langle t_1, t_3, t_4 \rangle$.

Definition 2.16 For a PT-net (N, M_0), a marking M is said to be *reachable*, in notation $M_0 [N,*\rangle M$, if and only if there exists a firable sequence σ such that $M_0 [N,\sigma\rangle M$. $[N, M_0\rangle$ represents the set of all reachable markings of (N, M_0).

When there is no confusion in the context, $M_0 [N,*\rangle M_n$ and $[N, M_0\rangle$ can be written as $M_0 [*\rangle M$ and $[M_0\rangle$ respectively. The reachable markings of a PT-net can be graphically represented by a *reachability graph*, where the nodes denote the reachable markings, and the arcs denote the changes of markings.

Example 2.8 For illustration of reachable markings, Fig. 2.6 shows another PT-net (N, M_0), where $M_0 = (1, 0, 1, 0, 0, 0)$. There are three other markings which are reachable from M_0. At M_0, on firing t_1, $M_1 = (0, 1, 0, 0, 0, 0)$ is reached, in notation, $M_0 [t_1\rangle M_1$. At M_0, on firing t_3, $M_2 = (1, 0, 0, 1, 1, 0)$ is reached, in notation, $M_0 [t_3\rangle M_2$. At M_2, on firing t_4, $M_3 = (1, 0, 0, 0, 1, 1)$ is reached, in notation, $M_0 [t_3, t_4\rangle M_3$. M_0 can be reached from M_1 on firing t_2, in notation, $M_1 [t_2\rangle M_0$. Also, M_0 can be

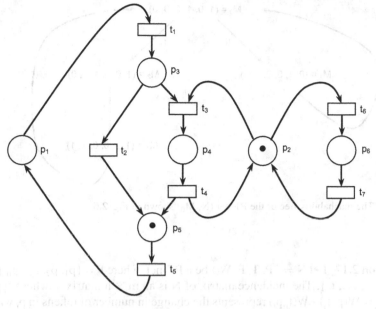

Fig. 2.5 A PT-net (N, M_3) obtained from (N, M_0) in Fig. 2.4 after firing $\langle\, t_1, t_3, t_4\,\rangle$

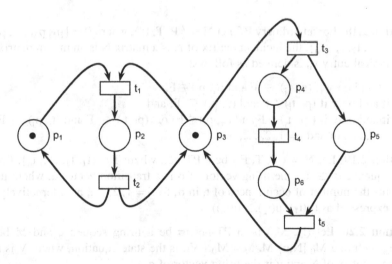

Fig. 2.6 A PT-net (N, M_0), where $M_0 = (1, 0, 1, 0, 0, 0)$

reached from M_3 on firing t_5, in notation, $M_3\,[t_5\rangle\,M_0$. Figure 2.7 shows the reachability tree of (N, M_0).

In the following, an incidence matrix is introduced for representing the token distribution on firing a transition in a PT-net. With the incidence matrix, a state equation is defined to show the markings before and after firing a transition or a sequence of transitions.

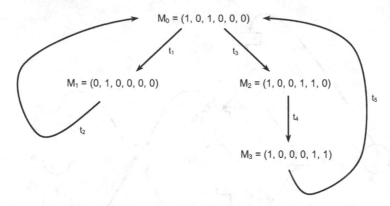

Fig. 2.7 The reachability tree of the PT-net (N, M_0) shown in Fig. 2.6

Definition 2.17 Let $N = \langle P, T, F, W \rangle$ be a PT-net, where $P = \{p_1, p_2, \ldots, p_m\}$ and $T = \{t_1, t_2, \ldots, t_n\}$. The incidence matrix of N is an $m \times n$ matrix V whose typical entry $v_{ij} = W(p_i, t_j) - W(t_j, p_i)$ represents the change in number of tokens in p_i when t_j fires once, for $i = 1, 2, \ldots, m$ and $j = 1, 2, \ldots, n$.

An alternative definition of the incidence matrix for an ordinary PT-net is given below.

Definition 2.18 For an ordinary PT-net $N = \langle P, T, F \rangle$, where $P = \{p_1, p_2, \ldots, p_m\}$ and $T = \{t_1, t_2, \ldots, t_n\}$, the incident matrix of N is a matrix N is an $m \times n$ matrix V whose typical entry v_{ij} is defined as follows:

$v_{ij} = -1$ if and only if $(p_i, t_j) \in F$ and $(t_i, p_j) \notin F$,
$v_{ij} = 1$ if and only if $(p_i, t_j) \notin F$ and $(t_i, p_j) \in F$, and
$v_{ij} = 0$ if and only if $((p_i, t_j) \notin F$ and $(t_i, p_j) \notin F)$ or $((p_i, t_j) \in F$ and $(t_i, p_j) \in F)$,
for $i = 1, 2, \ldots, m$ and $j = 1, 2, \ldots, n$.

Definition 2.19 Let $N = \langle P, T, F \rangle$ be a PT-net, where $T = \{t_1, t_2, \ldots, t_n\}$. For a firing sequence $\sigma \in T^+$, the firing vector of σ is a transition vector μ, where $\mu(t_i)$ represents the number of occurrences of t_i in σ, for $i = 1, 2, \ldots, n$. Alternatively, μ can be expressed as $(\mu(t_1), \mu(t_2), \ldots \mu(t_n))$.

Definition 2.20 Let (N, M_0) be a PT-net, σ be a firing sequence and M be a marking such that $M_0 [N, \sigma\rangle M$. $M = M_0 + V\mu$ is the state equation, where V is the incidence matrix of N and μ is the firing vector of σ.

Example 2.9 Consider the PT-net (N, M_0) shown in Fig. 2.4. $N = \langle P, T, F \rangle$, where $P = \{p_1, p_2, p_3, p_4, p_5, p_6\}$, $T = \{t_1, t_2, t_3, t_4, t_5, t_6, t_7\}$ and $F = \{(p_1, t_1), (t_5, p_1), (p_2, t_3), (p_2, t_6), (t_4, p_2), (t_7, p_2), (p_3, t_2), (p_3, t_3), (t_1, p_3), (p_4, t_4), (t_3, p_4), (p_5, t_5), (t_2, p_5), (t_4, p_5), (p_6, t_7), (t_6, p_6)\}$. Let V be the incidence matrix of N. V can be represented by a 6×7 matrix, as follows.

	t_1	t_2	t_3	t_4	t_5	t_6	t_7
p_1	-1	0	0	0	1	0	0
p_2	0	0	-1	1	0	-1	1
p_3	1	-1	-1	0	0	0	0
p_4	0	0	1	-1	0	0	0
p_5	0	1	0	1	-1	0	0
p_6	0	0	0	0	0	1	-1

The initial marking $M_0 = (1, 1, 0, 0, 0, 0)$ can be represented by a 6×1 matrix, as follows.

	M_0
p_1	1
p_2	1
p_3	0
p_4	0
p_5	0
p_6	0

Consider a firing sequence $\sigma = \langle t_1, t_3, t_4 \rangle$ for (N, M_0). Let $\mu = (1, 0, 1, 1, 0, 0, 0)$ be the firing vector for σ. μ can be represented by the following 7×1 matrix.

	μ
t_1	1
t_2	0
t_3	1
t_4	1
t_5	0
t_6	0
t_7	0

The state equation $M_0 + V\mu = M$ is shown below. A new marking $M = (0, 1, 0, 0, 1, 0)$. This corresponds to the PT-net shown in Fig. 2.5.

$$
\begin{vmatrix} 1 \\ 1 \\ 0 \\ 0 \\ 0 \\ 0 \end{vmatrix}
+
\begin{vmatrix} -1 & 0 & 0 & 0 & 1 & 0 & 0 \\ 0 & 0 & -1 & 1 & 0 & -1 & 1 \\ 1 & -1 & -1 & 0 & 0 & 0 & 0 \\ 0 & 0 & 1 & -1 & 0 & 0 & 0 \\ 0 & 1 & 0 & 1 & -1 & 0 & 0 \\ 0 & 0 & 0 & 0 & 0 & 1 & -1 \end{vmatrix}
\bullet
\begin{vmatrix} 1 \\ 0 \\ 1 \\ 1 \\ 0 \\ 0 \\ 0 \end{vmatrix}
=
\begin{vmatrix} 0 \\ 1 \\ 0 \\ 0 \\ 1 \\ 0 \end{vmatrix}
$$

Example 2.10 Consider the PT-net (N, M_0) shown in Fig. 2.6. Let V be the incidence matrix of N, as follows.

$$\begin{vmatrix} -1 & 1 & 0 & 0 & 0 \\ 1 & -1 & 0 & 0 & 0 \\ -1 & 1 & -1 & 0 & 1 \\ 0 & 0 & 1 & -1 & 0 \\ 0 & 0 & 1 & 0 & -1 \\ 0 & 0 & 0 & 1 & -1 \end{vmatrix}$$

For (N, M_0), $\sigma = \langle\, t_1, t_2, t_3, t_4, t_5, t_1, t_2, t_3, t_4 \,\rangle$ is a firable sequence at $M_0 = (1, 0, 1, 0, 0, 0)$. On firing σ, a new marking $M = (1, 0, 0, 0, 1, 1)$, in notation, $M_0 [t_1, t_2, t_3, t_4, t_5, t_1, t_2, t_3, t_4\rangle M$. This can be represented by the following state equation $M_0 + V\mu = M$.

$$\begin{vmatrix} 1 \\ 0 \\ 1 \\ 0 \\ 0 \\ 0 \end{vmatrix} + \begin{vmatrix} -1 & 1 & 0 & 0 & 0 \\ 1 & -1 & 0 & 0 & 0 \\ -1 & 1 & -1 & 0 & 1 \\ 0 & 0 & 1 & -1 & 0 \\ 0 & 0 & 1 & 0 & -1 \\ 0 & 0 & 0 & 1 & -1 \end{vmatrix} \bullet \begin{vmatrix} 2 \\ 2 \\ 2 \\ 2 \\ 1 \end{vmatrix} = \begin{vmatrix} 1 \\ 0 \\ 0 \\ 0 \\ 1 \\ 1 \end{vmatrix}$$

In the following, the place invariants and transition invariants of a PT-net are formally defined. The invariants are usually used in characterizing the properties of a PT-net.

Definition 2.21 For a PT-net $N = \langle\, P, T, F \,\rangle$, a place invariant is a place vector $\alpha \geq 0$ such that $\alpha V = 0$, where V is the incidence matrix of N.

Definition 2.22 For a PT-net $N = \langle\, P, T, F \,\rangle$, a transition invariant is a transition vector $\beta \geq 0$ such that $V\beta = 0$, where V is the incidence matrix of N.

Example 2.11 Consider the PT-net $N = \langle\, P, T, F \,\rangle$ shown in Fig. 2.6. Let $\alpha = (1, 2, 1, 1, 0, 1) \geq 0$ be a place vector. We have $\alpha V = 0$, where V is the incidence matrix of N, as shown below. Hence, α is a place invariant in N.

$$\begin{vmatrix} 1 & 2 & 1 & 1 & 0 & 1 \end{vmatrix} \bullet \begin{vmatrix} -1 & 1 & 0 & 0 & 0 \\ 1 & -1 & 0 & 0 & 0 \\ -1 & 1 & -1 & 0 & 1 \\ 0 & 0 & 1 & -1 & 0 \\ 0 & 0 & 1 & 0 & -1 \\ 0 & 0 & 0 & 1 & -1 \end{vmatrix} = \begin{vmatrix} 0 & 0 & 0 & 0 & 0 \end{vmatrix}$$

Let $\beta = (1, 1, 1, 1, 1) \geq 0$ be a transition vector. We have $V\beta = 0$, where V is the incidence matrix of N, as shown below. Hence, β is a transition invariant of N.

$$\begin{vmatrix} -1 & 1 & 0 & 0 & 0 \\ 1 & -1 & 0 & 0 & 0 \\ -1 & 1 & -1 & 0 & 1 \\ 0 & 0 & 1 & -1 & 0 \\ 0 & 0 & 1 & 0 & -1 \\ 0 & 0 & 0 & 1 & -1 \end{vmatrix} \bullet \begin{vmatrix} 1 \\ 1 \\ 1 \\ 1 \\ 1 \end{vmatrix} = \begin{vmatrix} 0 \\ 0 \\ 0 \\ 0 \\ 0 \\ 0 \end{vmatrix}$$

2.2 Properties of Petri Nets

The properties of a Petri net can be categorized as behavioural properties and structural properties. Behavioural properties are dependent on the initial marking in the sense that such properties hold for a specific initial marking. Structural properties are independent of the initial marking. These properties hold for any initial marking or are concerned with the existence of certain firing sequences from some initial markings.

2.2.1 Behavioural Properties

In the following, we define the behavioural properties of Petri nets, including liveness, deadlock freeness, boundedness, safeness and reversibility.

Definition 2.23 For a PT-net (N, M_0), a transition t is said to be live if and only if $\forall M \in [N, M_0\rangle, \exists M' : M [N, *\rangle M' [N, t\rangle$. (N, M_0) is said to be live if and only if every transition of (N, M_0) is live.

Definition 2.24 Let (N, M_0) be a PT-net, where $N = \langle P, T, F \rangle$. (N, M_0) is said to be deadlock-free if and only if $\forall M \in [N, M_0\rangle, \exists t \in T : M[N, t\rangle$.

It is obvious that liveness implies deadlock freeness. Hence, a live PT-net (N, M_0) is deadlock-free.

Definition 2.25 For a PT-net (N, M_0), a place p is said to be bounded (or k-bounded) if and only if there exists $k > 0$, such that $\forall M \in [N, M_0\rangle : M (p) \leq k$. (N, M_0) is said to be bounded (or k-bounded) if and only if every place is bounded (or k-bounded).

Definition 2.26 A PT-net (N, M_0) is said to be safe if and only if every place is 1-bounded.

Definition 2.27 A PT-net (N, M_0) is said to be reversible if and only if $\forall M \in [N, M_0\rangle : M [N,*\rangle M_0$.

Definition 2.28 A PT-net (N, M_0) is said to be well-behaved if and only if it is live, bounded and reversible.

Fig. 2.8 A PT-net (N, M_0)
which is neither live nor
reversible

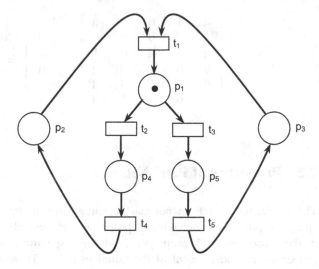

Example 2.12 Consider the PT-net (N, M_0) shown in Fig. 2.6. As earlier mentioned, besides the initial marking M_0, there are three reachable markings, $M_1 = (0, 1, 0, 0, 0, 0)$, $M_2 = (1, 0, 0, 1, 1, 0)$, and $M_3 = (1, 0, 0, 0, 1, 1)$.

Let us consider the liveness of the transitions. t_1, t_2, t_3, t_4 and t_5 are live since $M_0[t_1\rangle$, $M_1[t_2\rangle$, $M_0[t_3\rangle$, $M_2[t_4\rangle$ and $M_3[t_5\rangle$. Since every transition of (N, M_0) is live, (N, M_0) is live, and hence, deadlock free.

Let us consider the boundedness of the places. p_1, p_2, p_3, p_4, p_5 and p_6 are bounded and safe since $\forall M \in [N,M_0\rangle : M(p_1) \leq 1, M(p_2) \leq 1, M(p_3) \leq 1, M(p_4) \leq 1, M(p_5) \leq 1$, and $M(p_6) \leq 1$. Since every place of (N, M_0) is bounded and safe, (N, M_0) is bounded and safe.

(N, M_0) is also reversible since $M_1[t_2\rangle M_0$, $M_2[t_4, t_5\rangle M_0$ and $M_3[t_5\rangle M_0$. Therefore, (N, M_0) is a well-behaved PT-net.

Example 2.13 Figure 2.8 shows a PT-net (N, M_0), where $M_0 = (1, 0, 0, 0, 0)$. Besides the initial marking M_0, there are four reachable markings, $M_1 = (0, 0, 0, 1, 0)$, $M_2 = (0, 1, 0, 0, 0)$, $M_3 = (0, 0, 0, 0, 1)$, and $M_4 = (0, 0, 1, 0, 0)$.

Let us consider the liveness of t_1. There does not exist a reachable marking M such that $M[t_1\rangle$. t_1 is not live. Hence, (N, M_0) is not live.

For M_3, there does not exist a transition t such that $M_3[t\rangle$. Similarly, for M_4, there does not exist a transition t such that $M_4[t\rangle$. Hence, (N, M_0) is not deadlock-free. Deadlock would occur at the markings M_3 or M_4.

Let us consider the boundedness of the places. p_1, p_2, p_3, p_4 and p_5 are bounded and safe since $\forall M \in [N,M_0\rangle : M(p_1) \leq 1, M(p_2) \leq 1, M(p_3) \leq 1, M(p_4) \leq 1$ and $M(p_5) \leq 1$. Since every place of (N, M_0) is bounded and safe, (N, M_0) is bounded and safe.

Besides, (N, M_0) is not reversible since, for a reachable marking M_1, the condition $M_1 [N,*\rangle M_0$ does not hold.

Fig. 2.9 A PT-net (N, M_0) which is not bounded

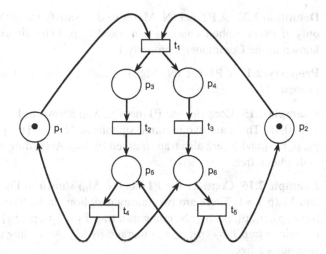

Example 2.14 Figure 2.9 shows another PT-net (N, M_0), where $M_0 = (1, 1, 0, 0, 0, 0)$. After firing $\langle t_1 \rangle$, a new marking $M_1 = (0, 0, 1, 1, 0, 0)$ is reached. At M_1, after firing $\langle t_2, t_3 \rangle$, a new marking $M_2 = (0, 0, 0, 0, 1, 1)$ is reached. Then, at M_2, after firing $\langle t_4, t_5 \rangle$, a new marking $M_3 = (1, 1, 0, 0, 1, 1)$ is reached. At M_3, after firing $\langle t_4, t_5 \rangle$ again, a new marking $M_4 = (2, 2, 0, 0, 1, 1)$ is reached. If firing $\langle t_4, t_5 \rangle$ repeatly, more and more tokens would be accumulated in p_1 and p_2. Obviously, p_1 and p_2 are not bounded. Hence, (N, M_0) is not bounded.

Let us consider the liveness of each transition. t_1 is live since $M_0[t_1\rangle$. t_2 is live since $M_1[t_2\rangle$. t_3 is live since $M_1[t_3\rangle$. t_4 is live since $M_2[t_4\rangle$. t_5 is live since $M_2[t_5\rangle$. Since every transition of (N, M_0) is live, (N, M_0) is live.

Besides, (N, M_0) is not reversible since, for a reachable marking M_1, the condition $M_1 [N,*\rangle M_0$ does not hold.

Siphons and traps were first introduced by Commoner [7]. Commoner defined a special property, called siphon-trap property or Commoner's property, for characterizing the deadlock freeness of a PT-net. For some subclasses of Petri nets, the siphon-trap property can also be used for characterizing the liveness and reversibility of a PT-net. In the following, we define siphons, traps and the siphon-trap property for a PT-net.

Definition 2.29 For a PT-net $N = \langle P, T, F \rangle$, a set of places $S \subseteq P$ is called a siphon if and only if $^\bullet S \subseteq S^\bullet$.

Definition 2.30 A siphon S of a PT-net N is said to be minimal if and only if there does not exist another siphon S' in N such that $S' \subset S$.

Definition 2.31 For a PT-net $N = \langle P, T, F \rangle$, a set of places $T \subseteq P$ is called a trap if and only if $T^\bullet \subseteq {}^\bullet T$.

Definition 2.32 Let T be a trap in a PT-net (N, M_0). T is said to be a marked trap if and only if $\forall p \in T : M_0(p) > 0$.

Definition 2.33 A PT-net (N, M_0) is said to satisfy the siphon-trap property if and only if every siphon contains a marked trap. (The siphon-trap property is also known as the Commoner's property.)

Property 2.1 A PT-net (N, M_0) is deadlock free if it satisfies the siphon-trap property [7–9].

Example 2.15 Consider the PT-net (N, M_0) shown in Fig. 2.6, where $M_0 = (1, 0, 1, 0, 0, 0)$. There are two minimal siphons in N, $S_1 = \{p_1, p_2\}$ and $S_2 = \{p_2, p_3, p_4, p_5, p_6\}$. S_1 and S_2 are also traps marked by M_0. According to Property 2.1, (N, M_0) is deadlock free.

Example 2.16 Consider the PT-net (N, M_0) shown in Fig. 2.9, where $M_0(p_1) = 1$ and $M_0(p_2) = 1$. There are two minimal siphons in N, $S_1 = \{p_1, p_3, p_4, p_5, p_6\}$ and $S_2 = \{p_2, p_3, p_4, p_5, p_6\}$. S_1 contains a trap $T_1 = \{p_1, p_3, p_5\}$ marked by M_0. S_2 also contains a trap $T_2 = \{p_2, p_4, p_6\}$ marked by M_0. According to Property 2.1, (N, M_0) is deadlock free.

The following property shows a sufficient condition for boundedness, based on place invariant.

Property 2.2 A PT-net (N, M_0) is bounded if there exist a place invariant α in N such that $\alpha > 0$ [4–6].

Example 2.17 Consider the (N, M_0) shown in Fig. 2.6. Let V be the incidence matrix of N. $\alpha = (1, 4, 3, 2, 1, 2) > 0$ is a place invariant since $\alpha V = 0$, as shown below. According to Property 2.2, (N, M_0) is bounded.

$$
\begin{vmatrix} 1 & 4 & 3 & 2 & 1 & 2 \end{vmatrix} \bullet
\begin{vmatrix}
-1 & 1 & 0 & 0 & 0 \\
1 & -1 & 0 & 0 & 0 \\
-1 & 1 & -1 & 0 & 1 \\
0 & 0 & 1 & -1 & 0 \\
0 & 0 & 1 & 0 & -1 \\
0 & 0 & 0 & 1 & -1
\end{vmatrix}
=
\begin{vmatrix} 0 & 0 & 0 & 0 & 0 \end{vmatrix}
$$

2.2.2 Structural Properties

In the following, we define the structural properties of Petri nets, including structural liveness, structural boundedness, well-formedness, consistency, repetitiveness and conservativeness. The algebraic characterizations of these properties are also provided.

Definition 2.34 A PT-net N is said to be structurally live if and only if there exists an initial marking M_0 such that (N, M_0) is live.

Fig. 2.10 A PT-net N
which is structurally live
and structurally bounded

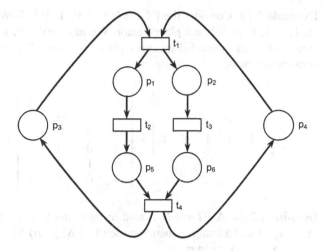

Definition 2.35 A PT-net N is said to be structurally bounded if and only if, for any initial marking M_0, (N, M_0) is bounded.

Algebraic Characterization 2.1 A PT-net $N = \langle P, T, F \rangle$ is structurally bounded if and only if there exists a place vector $\alpha > 0$ such that $\alpha V \leq 0$, where V is the incidence matrix of N.

Definition 2.36 A PT-net $\langle P, T, F \rangle$ is said to be conservative if and only if, for any initial marking M_0, $\forall M \in [N, M_0\rangle : M(P) = M_0(P)$, where $M(P)$ and $M_0(P)$ is the number of tokens at M and M_0 respectively.

Algebraic Characterization 2.2 A PT-net is said to be conservative if and only if there exists a place vector $\alpha > 0$ such that $\alpha V = 0$, where V is the incidence matrix of N.

According to the Algebraic Characterizations 2.1 and 2.2, conservativeness is a special case of structural boundedness. Hence, conservativeness implies structural boundedness.

Definition 2.37 A PT-net N is said to be well-formed if and only if there exists an initial marking M_0 such that (N, M_0) is live and bounded.

Example 2.18 Figure 2.10 shows a PT-net $N = \langle P, T, F \rangle$, where $P = \{p_1, p_2, p_3, p_4, p_5, p_6\}$ and $T = \{t_1, t_2, t_3, t_4\}$.

N is structurally live, since there exists an initial marking $M_0 = (1, 1, 0, 0, 0, 0)$, such that (N, M_0) is live. N is also structurally bounded, since, for any initial marking M_0, (N, M_0) is bounded.

For any initial marking M_0, every reachable marking from M_0 marks a constant number of tokens. N is conservative.

For N, there exists an initial marking $M_0 = (1, 1, 0, 0, 0, 0)$ such that (N, M_0) is live and bounded. Hence, N is well-formed.

Example 2.19 Consider the PT-net $N = \langle P, T, F \rangle$ shown in Fig. 2.10. Let $\alpha = (1, 1, 1, 1, 1, 1) > 0$ be a place vector. We have $\alpha V = 0$, where V is the incidence matrix of N, as shown below. α is a place invariant. N is structurally bounded and conservativeness.

$$\begin{vmatrix} 1 & 1 & 1 & 1 & 1 & 1 \end{vmatrix} \bullet \begin{vmatrix} 1 & -1 & 0 & 0 \\ 1 & 0 & -1 & 0 \\ -1 & 0 & 0 & 1 \\ -1 & 0 & 0 & 1 \\ 0 & 1 & 0 & -1 \\ 0 & 0 & 1 & -1 \end{vmatrix} = \begin{vmatrix} 0 & 0 & 0 & 0 \end{vmatrix}$$

Definition 2.38 A PT-net N is said to be consistent if and only if there exists a marking M and a firing sequence σ such that $M [N,\sigma\rangle M$ and every transition of N occurs at least once in σ.

Algebraic Characterization 2.3 A PT-net $N = \langle P, T, F \rangle$ is consistent if and only if there exists a transition vector $\beta > 0$ such that $V\beta = 0$, where V is the incidence matrix of N.

Definition 2.39 A PT-net N is said to be repetitive if and only if there exist a marking M and a firing sequence σ such that $M [N,\sigma\rangle$ and every transition of N occurs infinitely often in σ.

Algebraic Characterization 2.4 A PT-net $N = \langle P, T, F \rangle$ is repetitive if and only if there exists a transition vector $\beta > 0$ such that $V\beta \geq 0$, where V is the incidence matrix of N.

According to the Algebraic Characterizations 2.3 and 2.4, consistency is a special case of repetitiveness. Hence, consistency implies repetitiveness.

Example 2.20 Consider the PT-net $N = \langle P, T, F \rangle$ shown in Fig. 2.10. There exists a marking $M = (1, 1, 0, 0, 0, 0)$ and a firing sequence $\sigma = \langle t_2, t_3, t_4, t_1 \rangle$, such that $M [N,\sigma\rangle M$. Every transition of N occurs once in σ. Hence, N is consistent. N is also repetitive. There exists a firing sequence $\sigma' = \langle t_2, t_3, t_4, t_1, t_2, t_3, t_4, t_1, t_2, t_3, t_4, t_1, t_2, t_3, t_4, t_1, \ldots \rangle$ such that $M [N,\sigma'\rangle$ and every transition of N occurs infinitely often in σ'.

Example 2.21 Let us illustrate Algebraic Characterizations 2.3 and 2.4 using the PT-net $N = \langle P, T, F \rangle$ shown in Fig. 2.10. Let $\beta = (1, 1, 1, 1) > 0$ be a transition vector. We have $V\beta = 0$, where V is the incidence matrix of N, as shown below. Hence, N is consistent and repetitive.

$$\begin{vmatrix} 1 & -1 & 0 & 0 \\ 1 & 0 & -1 & 0 \\ -1 & 0 & 0 & 1 \\ -1 & 0 & 0 & 1 \\ 0 & 1 & 0 & -1 \\ 0 & 0 & 1 & -1 \end{vmatrix} \bullet \begin{vmatrix} 1 \\ 1 \\ 1 \\ 1 \end{vmatrix} = \begin{vmatrix} 0 \\ 0 \\ 0 \\ 0 \\ 0 \\ 0 \end{vmatrix}$$

2.3 State Machines and Their Properties

This section introduces a subclass of Petri nets, state machines.

Definition 2.40 A state machine is an ordinary PT-net $N = \langle P, T, F \rangle$, such that $\forall t \in T : |{}^\bullet t| = |t^\bullet| = 1$.

In this book, it is assumed that all state machines are connected. A state machine has the following known properties.

Property 2.3 A state machine (N, M_0) is live if and only if N is strongly connected and M_0 marks at least one place [5, 6].

Property 2.4 A live state machine (N, M_0) is bounded or k-bounded if and only if, for every place p, $M_0(p) \leq k$ [5, 6].

Example 2.22 Figure 2.11 shows a state machine (N, M_0), where $N = \langle P, T, F \rangle$, such that $\forall\, t \in T : |{}^\bullet t| = |t^\bullet| = 1$. N is strongly connected, and M_0 marks p_1. According to Property 2.3, (N, M_0) is live. According to Property 2.4, (N, M_0) is bounded (and safe).

Definition 2.41 A subnet $S = \langle P_S, T_S, F_S \rangle$ of a PT-net N is called a P-component of N if and only if S is a strongly connected state machine and $T_S = {}^\bullet P_S \cup P_S{}^\bullet$.

Definition 2.42 N is said to be P-coverable if and only if it is covered by a set of P-components.

Example 2.23 Figure 2.12 shows a PT-net $N = \langle P, T, F \rangle$, and two subnets of N, $S_1 = \langle P_1, T_1, F_1 \rangle$ and $S_2 = \langle P_2, T_2, F_2 \rangle$. S_1 is a P-component of N since S_1 is a strongly connected state machine and $T_1 = {}^\bullet P_1 \cup P_1{}^\bullet$. S_2 is also a P-component of N since S_2 is a strongly connected state machine and $T_2 = {}^\bullet P_2 \cup P_2{}^\bullet$. N is covered by S_1 and S_2 since $P = P_1 \cup P_2$, $T = T_1 \cup T_2$, and $F = F_1 \cup F_2$. Hence, N is P-coverable.

2.4 Marked Graphs and Their Properties

This section introduces another subclass of Petri nets, marked graphs.

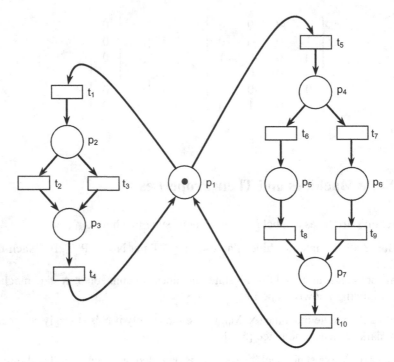

Fig. 2.11 A state machine

Definition 2.43 A marked graph is an ordinary PT-net $N = \langle P, T, F \rangle$, such that $\forall p \in P : | {}^{\bullet}p | = | p^{\bullet} | = 1$.

In this book, it is assumed that all marked graphs are connected. A marked graph has the following known properties.

Property 2.5 For a marked graph, the corresponding place vector of a cycle is a place invariant [5, 6, 10].

Property 2.6 A marked graph is conservative if every cycle is marked and every place belongs to a cycle.

Proof Let $N = \langle P, T, F \rangle$ be a marked graph, where $P = \{p_1, p_2, \ldots, p_n\}$. For each $p_i \in P$, p_i belongs to a cycle γ_i. According to Property 2.5, the corresponding place vector α_i of each γ_i is a place invariant of N, where $\alpha_i(p_i) > 0$. Then, $\alpha = \alpha_1 + \alpha_2 + \ldots + \alpha_n > 0$ is also a place invariant of N. N is conservative. □

Example 2.24 Figure 2.13 shows a marked graph (N, M_0), where $N = \langle P, T, F \rangle$ and $M_0 = (1, 1, 0, 0, 0, 0, 0, 0)$, such that $\forall p \in P : | {}^{\bullet}p | = | p^{\bullet} | = 1$. There are four cycles in N, $\gamma_1 = \langle p_1, p_4, p_6 \rangle$, $\gamma_2 = \langle p_1, p_5, p_7 \rangle$, $\gamma_3 = \langle p_2, p_3, p_4, p_6 \rangle$, and $\gamma_4 = \langle p_2, p_3, p_5, p_7 \rangle$. Each place belongs to a cycle. According to Property 2.5, the corresponding place vectors of γ_1, γ_2, γ_3 and γ_4, respectively $\alpha_1 = (1, 0, 0, 1, 0, 1, 0)$, $\alpha_2 = (1, 0, 0, 0, 1, 0, 1)$, $\alpha_3 = (0, 1, 1, 1, 0, 1, 0)$ and $\alpha_4 = (0, 1, 1, 0, 1, 0, 1)$, are

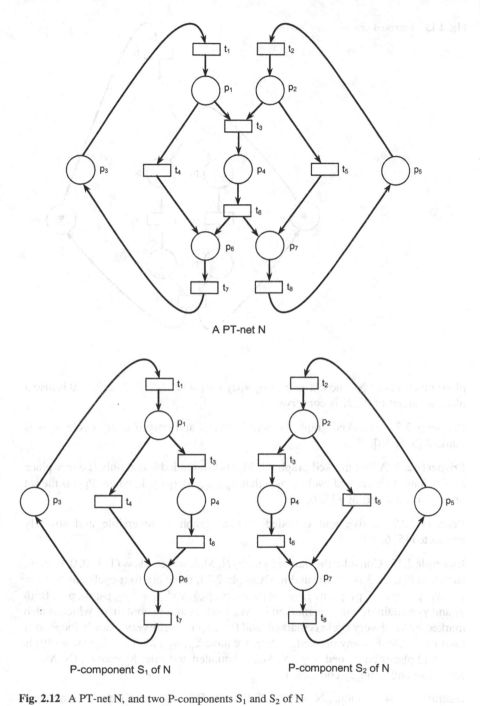

Fig. 2.12 A PT-net N, and two P-components S_1 and S_2 of N

Fig. 2.13 A marked graph

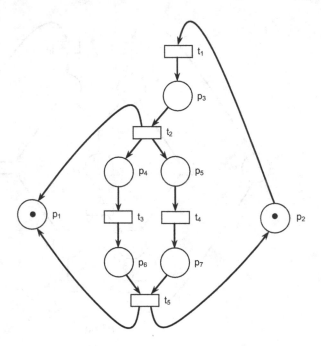

place invariants of N. Then, $\alpha = \alpha_1 + \alpha_2 + \alpha_3 + \alpha_4 = (2, 2, 2, 2, 2, 2, 2) > 0$ is also a place invariant of N. N is conservative.

Property 2.7 A marked graph (N, M_0) is live if and only if every cycle of N is marked [5, 6, 10].

Property 2.8 A live marked graph (N, M_0) is k-bounded if and only if every place in N belongs to a marked cycle γ such that $\Sigma_{p \in P[\gamma]} M_0(p) \leq k$, where $P[\gamma]$ is the set of places contained in γ [5, 6, 10].

Property 2.9 A live and bounded marked graph is reversible and strongly connected [5, 6, 10].

Example 2.25 Consider the marked graph (N, M_0), where $M_0 = (1, 1, 0, 0, 0, 0, 0)$, shown in Fig. 2.13 As illustrated in Example 2.24, there are four cycles in N, $\gamma_1 = \langle p_1, p_4, p_6 \rangle$, $\gamma_2 = \langle p_1, p_5, p_7 \rangle$, $\gamma_3 = \langle p_2, p_3, p_4, p_6 \rangle$, and $\gamma_4 = \langle p_2, p_3, p_5, p_7 \rangle$. Both γ_1 and γ_2 contain p_1 which is marked by M_0. Both γ_3 and γ_4 contain p_2 which is also marked by M_0. Every cycle is marked, and (N, M_0) is live. Every place belongs to at least one cycle. For any marked cycle γ, we have $\Sigma_{p \in P[\gamma]} M_0(p) \leq 1$, where $P[\gamma]$ is the set of places contained in γ. (N, M_0) is bounded and safe. Moreover, (N, M_0) is reversible and strongly connected.

Definition 2.44 A subnet $N' = \langle P', T', F' \rangle$ of a PT-net N is called a T-component of N if and only if N' is a strongly connected marked graph and $P' = {}^{\bullet}T' \cup T'^{\bullet}$. N is said to be T-coverable if and only if it is covered by a set of T-components.

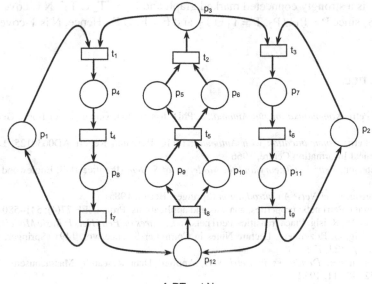

A PT-net N

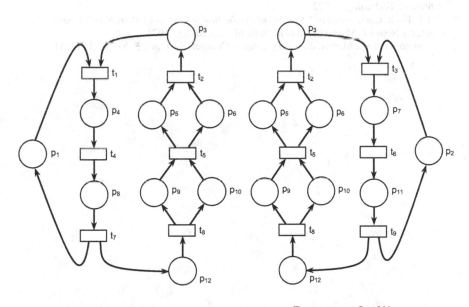

T-component S_1 of N   T-component S_2 of N

Fig. 2.14 A PT-net N, and two T-components S_1 and S_2 of N

Example 2.26 Figure 2.14 shows a PT-net N = ⟨ P, T, F ⟩, and two subnets of N, $S_1 = ⟨ P_1, T_1, F_1 ⟩$ and $S_2 = ⟨ P_2, T_2, F_2 ⟩$. S_1 is a T-component of N since S_1 is a strongly connected marked graph and $P_1 = {}^\bullet T_1 \cup T_1{}^\bullet$. S_2 is also a T-component of N since S_2 is a strongly connected marked graph and $P_2 = {}^\bullet T_2 \cup T_2{}^\bullet$. N is covered by S_1 and S_2 since $P = P_1 \cup P_2$, $T = T_1 \cup T_2$, and $F = F_1 \cup F_2$. Hence, N is T-coverable.

References

1. C.A. Petri, *Kommunikation mit Automaten*, PhD dissertation, University of Bonn, Germany, 1962
2. C.A. Petri, *Communication with Automata*, DTIC Research Report AD0630125, Defense Technical Information Centre, 1966
3. L. Peterson, *Petri Net Theory and the Modeling of System* (Prentice Hall, Englewood Cliffs, 1981)
4. W. Reisig, *Petri Nets: An Introduction* (Springer, Berlin, 1985)
5. T. Murata, Petri nets: properties, analysis and applications. Proc. IEEE **77**(4), 541–580 (1989)
6. J. Desel, W. Reisig, Place transition Petri nets, in *Lectures on Petri Nets I: Basic Models*, ed. by W. Reisig, G. Rozenberg. Lecture Notes in Computer Science, vol. 1491 (Springer, Berlin, 1998), pp. 122–173
7. F. Commoner, *Deadlocks in Petri Nets*, Applied Data Research, Massachusetts, Report CA-7206-2311, 1972
8. M.H.T. Hack, *Analysis of Production Schemata by Petri Nets*, MS Thesis, Massachusetts Institute of Technology, 1972
9. M.H.T. Hack, *Corrections to "Analysis of Production Schemata by Petri Nets"*, Computation Structures Note 17, Massachuesetts Institute of Technology, 1974
10. F. Commoner et al., Marked directed graphs. J. Comput. Syst. Sci. **5**, 511–523 (1971)

Part II
Theory of Augmented Marked Graphs

Chapter 3
Augmented Marked Graphs

This chapter provides a comprehensive description of augmented marked graphs and their properties. It starts with the basic definition and terminology of augmented marked graphs. Some special properties pertaining to cycles and siphons for augmented marked graphs are then discussed. These are followed by a detailed investigation of the liveness, reversibility, boundedness and conservativeness of augmented marked graphs. Algorithms for checking these properties are derived accordingly.

3.1 Definition and Terminology

Augmented marked graphs were first introduced by Chu as an extension of marked graphs for modelling systems with shared resources [1]. In an augmented marked graph, a set of special places are defined for representing the common resources. These special places are called resource places, which are initially marked. If removing the resource places and their associated arcs, an augmented marked graph would become a marked graph. A formal definition of augmented marked graphs is shown below.

Definition 3.1 An augmented marked graph $(N, M_0; R)$ is a PT-net (N, M_0) with a specific subset of places R satisfying the following conditions: (a) Every place in R is marked by M_0. (b) The PT-net (N', M_0') obtained from $(N, M_0; R)$ by removing the places in R and their associated arcs is a marked graph. (c) For each $r \in R$, there exist $k_r > 1$ pairs of transitions $D_r = \{ \langle t_{s1}, t_{h1} \rangle, \langle t_{s2}, t_{h2} \rangle, \ldots, \langle t_{skr}, t_{hkr} \rangle \}$ such that $r^{\bullet} = \{ t_{s1}, t_{s2}, \ldots, t_{skr} \} \subseteq T$, $^{\bullet}r = \{ t_{h1}, t_{h2}, \ldots, t_{hkr} \} \subseteq T$ and that, for each $\langle t_{si}, t_{hi} \rangle \in D_r$, there exists in N' an elementary path ρ_{ri} connecting t_{si} to t_{hi}. (d) In (N', M_0'), every cycle is marked and no ρ_{ri} is marked.

Example 3.1 Figure 3.1 shows an augmented marked graph $(N, M_0; R)$, where $R = \{ r_1, r_2 \}$ is the set of resource places. Figure 3.2 shows the PT-net (N', M_0') obtained

K.S. Cheung, *Augmented Marked Graphs*, DOI 10.1007/978-3-319-06428-4_3,
© Springer International Publishing Switzerland 2014

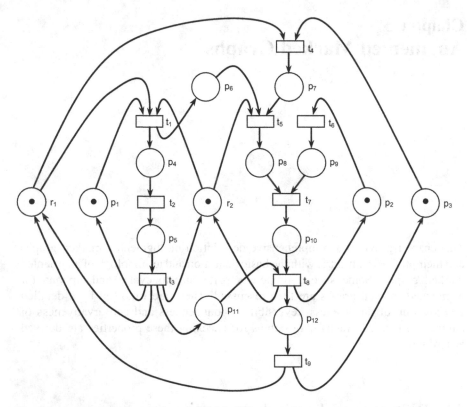

Fig. 3.1 An augmented marked graph $(N, M_0; R)$

from $(N, M_0; R)$ by removing the places in R and their associated arcs. (N', M_0') is a marked graph.

For $r_1 \in R$, there exist two pairs of transitions $D_{r1} = \{ \langle t_1, t_3 \rangle, \langle t_4, t_{10} \rangle \}$ such that $r_1^\bullet = \{ t_1, t_4 \}$ and $^\bullet r_1 = \{ t_3, t_{10} \}$, and that there exists an elementary path $\rho_{r11} = \langle t_1, p_4, t_2, p_5, t_3 \rangle$ connecting t_1 to t_3, and another elementary path $\rho_{r12} = \langle t_4, p_6, t_5, p_7, t_7, p_9, t_8, p_{11}, t_{10} \rangle$ connecting t_4 to t_{10}.

Similarly, for $r_2 \in R$, there exist two pairs of transitions $D_{r2} = \{ \langle t_1, t_3 \rangle, \langle t_5, t_8 \rangle \}$ such that $r_2^\bullet = \{ t_1, t_5 \}$ and $^\bullet r_2 = \{ t_3, t_8 \}$, and that there exists an elementary path $\rho_{r21} = \langle t_1, p_4, t_2, p_5, t_3 \rangle$ connecting t_1 to t_3, and another elementary path $\rho_{r22} = \langle t_5, p_7, t_7, p_3, t_8 \rangle$ connecting t_5 to t_8.

In (N', M_0'), every cycle is marked, and $\rho_{r11}, \rho_{r12}, \rho_{r21}$ and ρ_{r21} are not marked by M_0'.

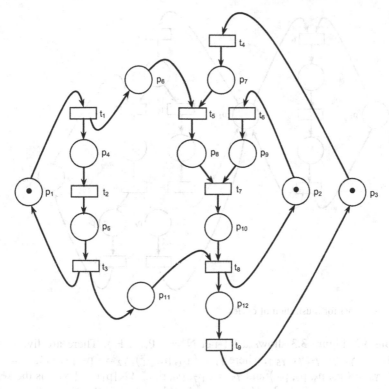

Fig. 3.2 A PT-net (N', M_0') obtained from $(N, M_0; R)$ in Fig. 3.1, by removing the places in R and their associated arcs

3.2 Cycles and Siphons in Augmented Marked Graphs

Augmented marked graphs possess some special properties pertaining to cycles and siphons [2–4]. In this section, the special properties of augmented marked graphs are investigated.

Definition 3.2 For a PT-net $N = \langle P, T, F \rangle$, Ω_N is defined as the set of all cycles in N, and $\Omega_N[p]$ as the set of cycles, each containing a place p.

For clarity in presentation, for a subset of places $S = \{ p_1, p_2, \ldots, p_n \}$ in a PT-net N, $\Omega_N[S] = (\Omega_N[p_1] \cup \Omega_N[p_2] \cup \ldots \cup \Omega_N[p_n])$ denotes the set of cycles, each containing at least one place in S.

Definition 3.3 Let $N = \langle P, T, F \rangle$ be a PT-net. For a set of cycles $Y \subseteq \Omega_N$, P[Y] denotes the set of places contained in Y, and $T[Y] = {}^\bullet P[Y] \cap P[Y]^\bullet$ denotes the set of transitions generated by Y.

For clarify in presentation, $P[\{\gamma\}]$ and $T[\{\gamma\}]$ can be written as $P[\gamma]$ and $T[\gamma]$, to denote the set of places contained in a cycle γ and the set of transitions generated by γ, respectively.

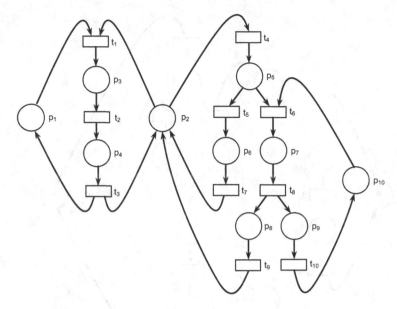

Fig. 3.3 A PT-net for illustration of cycles

Example 3.2 Figure 3.3 shows a PT-net $N = \langle P, T, F \rangle$. There are five cycles in N. $\Omega_N = \{ \gamma_1, \gamma_2, \gamma_3, \gamma_4, \gamma_5 \}$, where $\gamma_1 = \langle p_1, p_3, p_4 \rangle$, $\gamma_2 = \langle p_2, p_3, p_4 \rangle$, $\gamma_3 = \langle p_2, p_5, p_6 \rangle$, $\gamma_4 = \langle p_2, p_5, p_7, p_8 \rangle$ and $\gamma_5 = \langle p_7, p_9, p_{10} \rangle$. $\Omega_N[p_1] = \{ \gamma_1 \}$ is the set of cycles containing p_1. $\Omega_N[p_2] = \{ \gamma_2, \gamma_3, \gamma_4 \}$ is the set of cycles containing p_2.

Consider $Y_1 = \{ \gamma_1, \gamma_2, \gamma_3 \} \subseteq \Omega_N$. $P[Y_1] = \{ p_1, p_2, p_3, p_4, p_5, p_6 \}$ is the set of places contained in Y_1, where $\cdot P[Y_1] = \{ t_1, t_2, t_3, t_4, t_5, t_7, t_9 \}$ and $P[Y_1]\cdot = \{ t_1, t_2, t_3, t_4, t_5, t_6, t_7 \}$. $T[Y_1] = \cdot P[Y_1] \cap P[Y_1]\cdot = \{ t_1, t_2, t_3, t_4, t_5, t_7 \}$ is the set of transitions generated by Y_1.

Next, consider $Y_2 = \{ \gamma_3, \gamma_4, \gamma_5 \} \subseteq \Omega_N$. $P[Y_2] = \{ p_2, p_5, p_6, p_7, p_8, p_9, p_{10} \}$ is the set of places contained in Y_2, where $\cdot P[Y_2] = \{ t_3, t_4, t_5, t_6, t_7, t_8, t_9, t_{10} \}$ and $P[Y_2]\cdot = \{ t_1, t_4, t_5, t_6, t_7, t_8, t_9, t_{10} \}$. $T[Y_2] = \cdot P[Y_2] \cap P[Y_2]\cdot = \{ t_4, t_5, t_6, t_7, t_8, t_9, t_{10} \}$ is the set of transitions generated by Y_2.

Definition 3.4 In a PT-net $N = \langle P, T, F \rangle$, an elementary path $\rho = \langle x_1, x_2, \ldots, x_n \rangle$ is said to be conflict-free if and only if, for any $x_i \in T$ and $x_j \in P$ in ρ, $j \neq (i - 1) \Rightarrow x_j \notin \cdot x_i$.

Definition 3.5 For a PT-net N, a set of cycles $Y \subseteq \Omega_N$ is said to be conflict-free if and only if, for any $p_i, p_j \in P[Y]$, there exists in $P[Y]$ a conflict-free path from p_i to p_j.

Example 3.3 Figure 3.4 shows a PT-net $N = \langle P, T, F \rangle$. Consider the cycles in N that contains p_3. Let $\gamma_1, \gamma_2, \gamma_3 \in \Omega_N[p_3]$, where $\gamma_1 = \langle p_3, p_2, p_7 \rangle$, $\gamma_2 = \langle p_3, p_4 \rangle$ and $\gamma_3 = \langle p_3, p_1, p_6, p_{10}, p_8 \rangle$.

Consider $Y_1 = \{ \gamma_1, \gamma_2 \} \subseteq \Omega_N[p_3]$. For any $p_i, p_j \in P[Y_1] = \{ p_2, p_3, p_4, p_7 \}$, there exists a conflict-free path in Y_1 that connects p_i to p_j. For example, there exists

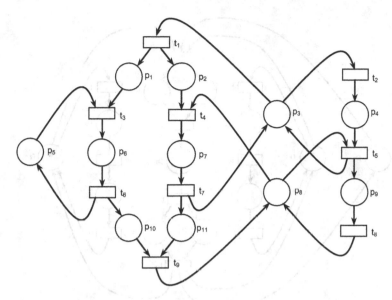

Fig. 3.4 A PT-net for illustration of conflict-free path

a conflict-free path $\langle p_2, t_4, p_7, t_7, p_3 \rangle$ that connects p_2 to p_3, a conflict-free path $\langle p_2, t_4, p_7, t_7, p_3, t_2, p_4 \rangle$ that connects p_2 to p_4, and a conflict-free path $\langle p_3, t_1, p_2, t_4, p_7 \rangle$ that connects p_3 and p_7. Hence, Y_1 is conflict-free.

Next, consider $Y_2 = \{ \gamma_2, \gamma_3 \} \subseteq \Omega_N[p_3]$. Y_2 is not conflict-free. We have $p_4, p_8 \in P[Y_2]$. p_4 is connected to p_8 via only one path $\rho = \langle p_4, t_5, p_3, t_1, p_1, t_3, p_6, t_6, p_{10}, t_9, p_8 \rangle$ in Y_2, and ρ is not conflict-free because $p_4, p_8 \in {}^\bullet t_5$.

Lemma 3.1 Let S be a minimal siphon in a PT-net. For any $p_i, p_j \in S$, there exists in S a conflict-free path from p_i to p_j [5].

Property 3.1 Let $(N, M_0; R)$ be an augmented marked graph. For a minimal siphon S in $(N, M_0; R)$, there exists a set of cycles $Y \subseteq \Omega_N$ such that $P[Y] = S$.

Proof Let $S = \{ p_1, p_2, \ldots, p_n \}$. For each p_i, ${}^\bullet p_i \neq \varnothing$, and there exists $p_j \in S$, where $p_j \neq p_i$, such that $(p_j^\bullet \cap {}^\bullet p_i) \neq \varnothing$. Since S is a minimal siphon, according to Lemma 3.1, p_i connects to p_j via a conflict-free path in S. Since p_j connects to p_i, this forms a cycle γ_i in S, where $p_i \in P[\gamma_i] \subseteq S$. Let $Y = \{ \gamma_1, \gamma_2, \ldots, \gamma_n \}$. We have $P[Y] = P[\gamma_1] \cup P[\gamma_2] \cup \ldots \cup P[\gamma_n] \subseteq S$. On the other hand, since $S = \{ p_1, p_2, \ldots, p_n \}$, $S \subseteq (P[\gamma_1] \cup P[\gamma_2] \cup \ldots \cup P[\gamma_n]) = P[Y]$. Hence, $P[Y] = S$. $\square$

Example 3.4 Figure 3.5 shows an augmented marked graph $(N, M_0; R)$. $S_1 = \{ r_1, p_2, p_3, p_6, p_7, p_9 \}$ is a minimal siphon. These exists $Y_1 = \{ \gamma_{11}, \gamma_{12} \} \subseteq \Omega_N$, where $\gamma_{11} = \langle r_1, p_2, p_6 \rangle$ and $\gamma_{12} = \langle r_1, p_3, p_7, p_9 \rangle$, such that $P[Y_1] = S_1 = \{ r_1, p_2, p_3, p_6, p_7, p_9 \}$. $S_2 = \{ r_1, p_2, p_4, p_6, p_7, p_{10} \}$ is another minimal siphon. These also exists $Y_2 = \{ \gamma_{21}, \gamma_{22} \} \subseteq \Omega_N$, where $\gamma_{21} = \langle r_1, p_2, p_6 \rangle$ and $\gamma_{22} = \langle r_1, p_4, p_7, p_{10} \rangle$, such that $P[Y_2] = S_2 = \{ r_1, p_2, p_4, p_6, p_7, p_{10} \}$.

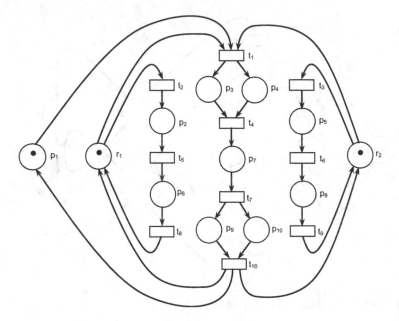

Fig. 3.5 An augmented marked graph for illustration of siphons

Property 3.2 Let S be a minimal siphon of an augmented marked graph $(N, M_0; R)$. For every place $p \in S$, there exists a set of cycles $Y \subseteq \Omega_N[p]$ such that Y is conflict free, $P[Y] \subseteq S$ and $\,^\bullet p \subseteq T[Y]$.

Proof Since $p \in S$, there exists a set of places $Q = \{ p_1, p_2, \ldots, p_n \} \subseteq S$, such that $\,^\bullet p \subseteq Q^\bullet$. For each p_i, according to Lemma 3.1, p is connected to p_i by a conflict-free path in S, thus forming a cycle $\gamma_i \in \Omega_N[p]$, where $P[\gamma_i] \subseteq S$. Then, we have $Y = \{ \gamma_1, \gamma_2, \ldots, \gamma_n \} \subseteq \Omega_N[p]$, such that $P[Y] = (P[\gamma_1] \cup P[\gamma_2] \cup \ldots \cup P[\gamma_n]) \subseteq S$ and Y is conflict-free. Since S is a siphon, $\,^\bullet p \subseteq (\,^\bullet S \cap S^\bullet) = (\,^\bullet P[Y] \cap P[Y]^\bullet) = T[Y]$. $\square$

Property 3.3 Every cycle in an augmented marked graph is marked.

Proof (by contradiction) Let $(N, M_0; R)$ be an augmented marked graph. Suppose there exists a cycle γ such that γ is not marked. γ does not contain any place in R. γ also exists in the PT-net (N', M_0') obtained from $(N, M_0; R)$ after removing the places in R and their associated arcs. However, by definition of augmented marked graphs, γ is marked. $\square$

Property 3.4 Every siphon in an augmented marked graph is marked.

Proof It follows from Properties 3.1 and 3.3 that every minimal siphon in an augmented marked graph is marked. Hence, every siphon, which contains at least one minimal siphon, is marked. $\square$

Example 3.5 Consider the augmented marked graph $(N, M_0; R)$, shown in Fig. 3.5. There are 12 minimal siphons, $S_1 = \{ p_1, p_3, p_7, p_9 \}$, $S_2 = \{ p_1, p_3, p_7,$

p_{10} }, $S_3 = \{ p_1, p_4, p_7, p_9 \}$, $S_4 = \{ p_1, p_4, p_7, p_{10} \}$, $S_5 = \{ r_1, p_2, p_3, p_6, p_7, p_9 \}$, $S_6 = \{ r_1, p_2, p_3, p_6, p_7, p_{10} \}$, $S_7 = \{ r_1, p_2, p_4, p_6, p_7, p_9 \}$, $S_8 = \{ r_1, p_2, p_4, p_6, p_7, p_{10} \}$, $S_9 = \{ r_2, p_3, p_5, p_7, p_8, p_9 \}$, $S_{10} = \{ r_2, p_3, p_5, p_7, p_8, p_{10} \}$, $S_{11} = \{ r_2, p_4, p_5, p_7, p_8, p_9 \}$ and $S_{12} = \{ r_2, p_4, p_5, p_7, p_8, p_{10} \}$. All of them are marked.

Property 3.5 Let $(N, M_0; R)$ be an augmented marked graph. For every $r \in R$, there exists a minimal siphon which contains only one marked place r.

Proof For each $r \in R$, let $D_r = \{ \langle t_{s1}, t_{h1} \rangle, \langle t_{s2}, t_{h2} \rangle, \ldots, \langle t_{sn}, t_{hn} \rangle \}$, where $r^{\bullet} = \{ t_{s1}, t_{s2}, \ldots, t_{sn} \}$ and ${}^{\bullet}r = \{ t_{h1}, t_{h2}, \ldots, t_{hn} \}$. For each $\langle t_{si}, t_{hi} \rangle \in D_r$, t_{si} connects to t_{hi} via an elementary path ρ_i which is not marked. Let $S = P_1 \cup P_2 \cup \ldots \cup P_n \cup \{ r \}$, where P_i is the set of places in ρ_i. For each $p \in P_i$, $|{}^{\bullet}p| = |p^{\bullet}| = 1$. Then, $({}^{\bullet}P_1 \cup {}^{\bullet}P_2 \cup \ldots \cup {}^{\bullet}P_n) \subseteq (P_1{}^{\bullet} \cup P_2{}^{\bullet} \cup \ldots \cup P_n{}^{\bullet} \cup r^{\bullet})$. Besides, ${}^{\bullet}r = \{ t_{h1}, t_{h2}, \ldots, t_{hn} \} \subseteq (P_1{}^{\bullet} \cup P_2{}^{\bullet} \cup \ldots \cup P_n{}^{\bullet})$. Hence, ${}^{\bullet}S = ({}^{\bullet}P_1 \cup {}^{\bullet}P_2 \cup \ldots \cup {}^{\bullet}P_n \cup {}^{\bullet}r) \subseteq (P_1{}^{\bullet} \cup P_2{}^{\bullet} \cup \ldots \cup P_n{}^{\bullet} \cup r^{\bullet}) = S^{\bullet}$. Therefore, S is a siphon in which r is the only one marked place. Let S' be a minimal siphon in S. According to Property 3.3, S' is marked. Since r is the only one marked place in S, r is also the only one marked place in S'. □

Example 3.6 Figure 3.6 shows an augmented marked graph $(N, M_0; R)$, where $R = \{ r_1, r_2 \}$. $S_1 = \{ r_1, p_2, p_4, p_6, p_7, p_9 \}$ is a minimal siphon. There exists $Y_1 = \{ \gamma_{11}, \gamma_{12} \} \subseteq \Omega_N$, where $\gamma_{11} = \langle r_1, p_4, p_7 \rangle$ and $\gamma_{12} = \langle r_1, p_2, p_6, p_9 \rangle$, such that $S_1 = P[Y_1]$ and ${}^{\bullet}r_1 = \{ t_9, t_{11} \} \subseteq T(Y_1)$. $r_1 \in R$ is the only one marked place in S_1.

$S_2 = \{ r_2, p_3, p_5, p_6, p_8, p_{10} \}$ is another minimal siphon. There exists $Y_2 = \{ \gamma_{21}, \gamma_{22} \} \subseteq \Omega_N$, where $\gamma_{21} = \langle r_2, p_5, p_8 \rangle$ and $\gamma_{22} = \langle r_2, p_3, p_6, p_{10} \rangle$, such that $S_2 = P[Y_2]$ and ${}^{\bullet}r_2 = \{ t_{10}, t_{11} \} \subseteq T(Y_2)$. $r_2 \in R$ is the only one marked place in S_2.

We define two categories of minimal siphons for augmented marked graphs, namely, R-siphons and NR-siphons.

Definition 3.6 For an augmented marked graph $(N, M_0; R)$, a minimal siphon is called a R-siphon if and only if it contains at least one place in R.

Definition 3.7 For an augmented marked graph $(N, M_0; R)$, a minimal siphon is called a NR-siphon if and only if it does not contain any place in R.

For augmented marked graphs, there are some special properties pertaining to R-siphons and NR-siphons. These special properties are useful in investigating the liveness and reversibility of augmented marked graphs.

Property 3.6 For an augmented marked graph $(N, M_0; R)$, a R-siphon is covered by a set of cycles $Y \subseteq \Omega_N[R]$.

Proof (By contradiction) Let S be a R-siphon. According to Property 3.1, S is covered by cycles. Suppose there exists a cycle γ in S, such that $\gamma \notin \Omega_N[R]$. By definition of augmented marked graphs, for any $p \in P[\gamma]$, $|{}^{\bullet}p| = |p^{\bullet}| = 1$. Hence, ${}^{\bullet}P[\gamma] = P[\gamma]^{\bullet}$, and $P[\gamma]$ is a siphon. Since there exists a place $r \in R$ such that $r \in S$ but $r \notin P[\gamma]$, we have $P[\gamma] \subset S$. However, since S is a minimal siphon, there does not exists any siphon $S' = P[\gamma] \subset S$. □

Example 3.7 Figure 3.7 shows an augmented marked graph $(N, M_0; R)$, where $R = \{ r_1, r_2 \}$. There are five minimal siphons, $S_1 = \{ r_1, p_3, p_4, p_7, p_8 \}$, $S_2 = \{ r_1, p_3, p_5, $

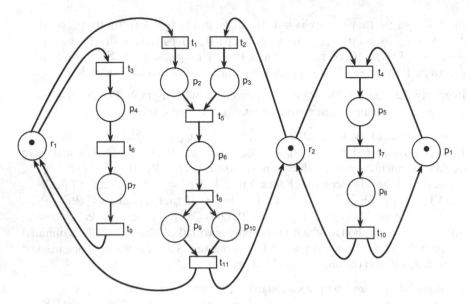

Fig. 3.6 Another augmented marked graph for illustration of siphons

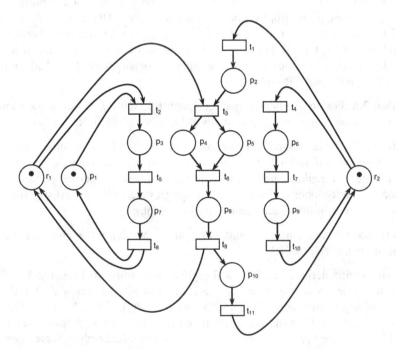

Fig. 3.7 An augmented marked graph for illustration of R-siphons and NR-siphons

p_7, p_8 }, $S_3 = \{ r_2, p_2, p_4, p_6, p_8, p_9, p_{10} \}$, $S_4 = \{ r_2, p_2, p_5, p_6, p_8, p_9, p_{10} \}$ and $S_5 = \{ p_1, p_3, p_7 \}$. S_1, S_2, S_3 and S_4 are R-siphons since they contain either r_1 or r_2. S_5 is a NR-siphon since it contains neither r_1 nor r_2.

For (N, M_0; R), every R-siphon is covered by a set of cycles in $\Omega_N[R]$. For example, S_1 is covered by $Y_1 = \{ \gamma_{11}, \gamma_{12} \} \subseteq \Omega_N[R]$, where $\gamma_{11} = \langle r_1, p_3, p_7 \rangle$ and $\gamma_{12} = \langle r_1, p_4, p_8 \rangle$. S_2 is covered by $Y_2 = \{ \gamma_{21}, \gamma_{22} \} \subseteq \Omega_N[R]$, where $\gamma_{21} = \langle r_1, p_3, p_7 \rangle$ and $\gamma_{12} = \langle r_1, p_5, p_8 \rangle$. S_3 is covered by $Y_3 = \{ \gamma_{31}, \gamma_{32} \} \subseteq \Omega_N[R]$, where $\gamma_{31} = \langle r_2, p_2, p_4, p_8, p_{10} \rangle$ and $\gamma_{32} = \langle r_2, p_8, p_9 \rangle$. S_4 is covered by $Y_4 = \{ \gamma_{41}, \gamma_{42} \} \subseteq \Omega_N[R]$, where $\gamma_{41} = \langle r_2, p_2, p_5, p_8, p_{10} \rangle$ and $\gamma_{42} = \langle r_2, p_8, p_9 \rangle$.

Property 3.7 Let S be a R-siphon of an augmented marked graph (N, M_0; R). For every $t \in (S^{\bullet} \setminus {}^{\bullet}S)$, there does not exist any place $p \in (S \setminus R)$ such that $t \in p^{\bullet}$.

Proof (by contradiction) Suppose there exists $s \in (S \setminus R)$ such that $t \in s^{\bullet}$. By definition of augmented marked graphs, $| {}^{\bullet}s | = | s^{\bullet} | = 1$. S is covered by cycles in accordance with Property 3.1. Hence, t is the one and only one transition in $s^{\bullet}$, where $t \in T[Y] = (S^{\bullet} \cap {}^{\bullet}S)$. This however contradicts $t \in (S^{\bullet} \setminus {}^{\bullet}S)$. $\square$

Property 3.8 For an augmented marked graph (N, M_0; R), a NR-siphon contains itself as a marked trap.

Proof Let S be a NR-siphon. According to Property 3.3, S is marked. It follows from the definition of augmented marked graphs that, for any $p \in S, | {}^{\bullet}p | = | p^{\bullet} | = 1$. Then, ${}^{\bullet}S = S^{\bullet}$ and S is also a trap. Hence, S contains itself as a marked trap. $\square$

Example 3.8 Consider the augmented marked graph (N, M_0; R) shown in Fig. 3.7. As illustrated in Example 3.7, $S_1 = \{ r_1, p_3, p_4, p_7, p_8 \}$ is a R-siphon. Then, $S_1^{\bullet} \setminus {}^{\bullet}S_1 = \{ t_{10} \}$. We have $S_1 \setminus R = \{ p_3, p_4, p_7, p_8 \}$, where $p_3^{\bullet} = \{ t_5 \}, p_4^{\bullet} = \{ t_6 \}, p_7^{\bullet} = \{ t_8 \}$, and $p_8^{\bullet} = \{ t_9 \}$. There does not exist any place $p \in (S \setminus R)$, such that $t_{10} \in p^{\bullet}$. As illustrated in Example 3.7, $S_5 = \{ p_1, p_3, p_7 \}$ is a NR-siphon. S_5 itself is also a trap marked by M_0.

3.3 Liveness and Reversibility of Augmented Marked Graphs

In the literature, the liveness and reversibility of augmented marked graphs were mainly studied by Chu [1] and Cheung [2–4]. Siphon-based characterizations and cycle-based charcterizations are reported.

This section investigates the liveness and reversibility of augmented marked graphs. It starts with the siphon-based characterizations. A cycle-inclusion property is then introduced, and the cycle-based characterizations would follow. Based on these characterizations, algorithms for checking the liveness and reversibility of augmented marked graphs are derived.

Property 3.9 An augmented marked graph is live if and only if every minimal siphon would never become empty [1].

Property 3.10 A augmented marked graph is reversible if it it live [1].

Property 3.11 An augmented marked graph is live and reversible if and only if every minimal siphon would never become empty.

Proof It simply follows Properties 3.9 and 3.10. □

Property 3.12 An augmented marked graph is live and reversible if and only if every R-siphon would never become empty.

Proof It simply follows Properties 3.8, 3.9 and 3.10. □

Property 3.13 An augmented marked graph is live and reversible if it satisfies the siphon-trap property [1].

Property 3.14 An augmented marked graph $(N, M_0; R)$ is live and reversible if every R-siphon contains a trap marked by M_0 [1].

Example 3.9 Consider the augmented marked graph $(N, M_0; R)$, where $R = \{ r_1, r_2 \}$, shown in Fig. 3.5. As illustrated in Example 3.5, there are 12 minimal siphons in $(N, M_0; R)$. $S_1 = \{ p_1, p_3, p_7, p_9 \}$, $S_2 = \{ p_1, p_3, p_7, p_{10} \}$, $S_3 = \{ p_1, p_4, p_7, p_9 \}$ and $S_4 = \{ p_1, p_4, p_7, p_{10} \}$ are NR-siphons. $S_5 = \{ r_1, p_2, p_3, p_6, p_7, p_9 \}$, $S_6 = \{ r_1, p_2, p_3, p_6, p_7, p_{10} \}$, $S_7 = \{ r_1, p_2, p_4, p_6, p_7, p_9 \}$, $S_8 = \{ r_1, p_2, p_4, p_6, p_7, p_{10} \}$, $S_9 = \{ r_2, p_3, p_5, p_7, p_8, p_9 \}$, $S_{10} = \{ r_2, p_3, p_5, p_7, p_8, p_{10} \}$, $S_{11} = \{ r_2, p_4, p_5, p_7, p_8, p_9 \}$ and $S_{12} = \{ r_2, p_4, p_5, p_7, p_8, p_{10} \}$ are R-siphons. Every minimal siphon contains a marked trap, and hence, would never become empty. $(N, M_0; R)$ is live and reversible. According to Property 3.14, we may consider only the R-siphons, $S_5, S_6, S_7, S_8, S_9, S_{10}, S_{11}$ and S_{12}.

Example 3.10 Consider the augmented marked graph $(N, M_0; R)$, where $R = \{ r_1, r_2 \}$, shown in Fig. 3.7. As illustrated in Example 3.7, there are five minimal siphons in $(N, M_0; R)$. $S_1 = \{ r_1, p_3, p_4, p_7, p_8 \}$, $S_2 = \{ r_1, p_3, p_5, p_7, p_8 \}$, $S_3 = \{ r_2, p_2, p_4, p_6, p_8, p_9, p_{10} \}$ and $S_4 = \{ r_2, p_2, p_5, p_6, p_8, p_9, p_{10} \}$ are R-siphons. $S_5 = \{ p_1, p_3, p_7 \}$ is a NR-siphon. Every minimal siphon contains a marked trap, and hence, would never become empty. $(N, M_0; R)$ is live and reversible. According to Property 3.14, we may consider only the R-siphons, we may consider only R-siphons, S_1, S_2, S_3 and S_{14}.

Based on Properties 3.6, 3.12 and 3.14, we derive a strategy for checking the liveness and reversibility of an augmented marked graph, as shown in Algorithm 3.1. Only the R-siphons are considered. After identifying the R-siphons based on cycles, we check whether each of them contains a marked trap or would eventually become empty.

Algorithm 3.1 Checking the liveness and reversibility of an augmented marked graph $(N, M_0; R)$.

Fig. 3.8 A PT-net for illustration of cycle inclusion property

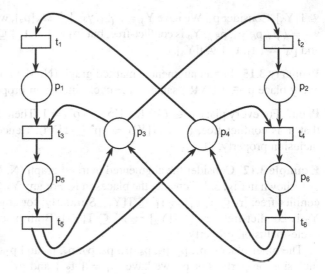

Step 1. Find all R-siphons based on $\Omega_N[R]$.

Step 2. Check if every R-siphon contains a marked trap. If yes, report $(N, M_0; R)$ is live and reversible. Otherwise, go to Step 3.

Step 3. For each R-siphon which does not contain any marked trap, check if it would never become empty. If yes, report $(N, M_0; R)$ is live and reversible. Otherwise, report $(N, M_0; R)$ is neither live nor reversible.

In the following, we define another property, called cycle-inclusion property, for augmented marked graphs. Proposed by Cheung, the cycle-inclusion property can be used for characterizing the siphon-trap property, and hence the liveness and reversibility, of augmented marked graphs [2–4].

Definition 3.8 For a PT-net $N = \langle P, T, F \rangle$, a place $p \in P$ is said to satisfy the cycle-inclusion property if and only if, for any set of cycles $Y \subseteq \Omega_N[p]$ such that Y is conflict-free, ${}^\bullet p \subseteq T[Y] \Rightarrow p^\bullet \subseteq T[Y]$.

Example 3.11 Figure 3.8 shows a PT-net $N = \langle P, T, F \rangle$, where $P = \{ p_1, p_2, p_3, p_4, p_5, p_6 \}$. The places p_1, p_2, p_5 and p_6 satisfy the cycle-inclusion property. Consider p_1. We have $\Omega_N[p_1] = \{ \gamma_{11}, \gamma_{12} \}$, where $\gamma_{11} = \langle p_4, p_1, p_5 \rangle$ and $\gamma_{12} = \langle p_4, p_1, p_5, p_3, p_2, p_6 \rangle$. For any $Y_1 \subseteq \Omega_N[p_1]$ such that Y_1 is conflict-free, ${}^\bullet p_1 = \{ t_1 \} \subseteq T[Y_1]$ and $p_1^\bullet = \{ t_3 \} \subseteq T[Y_1]$. Consider p_2. We have $\Omega_N[p_2] = \{ \gamma_{21}, \gamma_{22} \}$, where $\gamma_{21} = \langle p_3, p_2, p_6 \rangle$ and $\gamma_{22} = \langle p_3, p_2, p_6, p_4, p_1, p_5 \rangle$. For any $Y_2 \subseteq \Omega_N[p_2]$ such that Y_2 is conflict-free, ${}^\bullet p_2 = \{ t_2 \} \subseteq T[Y_2]$ and $p_2^\bullet = \{ t_4 \} \subseteq T[Y_2]$. The same property applies to p_5 and p_6.

The places p_3 and p_4 do not satisfy the cycle-inclusion property. Consider p_3. We have $Y_3 = \{ \gamma_{31}, \gamma_{32} \} \subseteq \Omega_N[p_3]$, where $\gamma_{31} = \langle p_3, p_5 \rangle$ and $\gamma_{32} = \langle p_3, p_5, p_4, p_6 \rangle$. Y_3 is conflict-free. However, ${}^\bullet p_3 = \{ t_5, t_6 \} \subseteq T[Y_3] = \{ t_3, t_4, t_5, t_6 \}$ and $p_3^\bullet = \{ t_2, t_3 \}$

$\nsubseteq T[Y_3]$. Consider p_4. We have $Y_4 = \{ \gamma_{41}, \gamma_{42} \} \subseteq \Omega_N[p_4]$, where $\gamma_{41} = \langle p_4, p_6 \rangle$ and $\gamma_{42} = \langle p_4, p_6, p_3, p_5 \rangle$. Y_4 is conflict-free, but ${}^{\bullet}p_4 = \{ t_5, t_6 \} \subseteq T[Y_4] = \{ t_3, t_4, t_5, t_6 \}$ and $p_4^{\bullet} = \{ t_1, t_4 \} \nsubseteq t[Y_4]$.

Property 3.15 For an augmented marked graph $(N, M_0; R)$, where $N = \langle P, T, F \rangle$, every place $p \in (P \setminus R)$ satisfies the cycle-inclusion property.

Proof For every place $p \in (P \setminus R)$, $| {}^{\bullet}p | = | p^{\bullet} | = 1$. Then, for any $Y \subseteq \Omega_N[p]$ such that Y is conflict free, $({}^{\bullet}p \subseteq T[Y]) \Rightarrow (p^{\bullet} \subseteq T[Y])$. Hence, p satisfies the cycle-inclusion property. $\square$

Example 3.12 Consider the augmented marked graph $(N, M_0; R)$, where $R = \{ r_1, r_2 \}$, shown in Fig. 3.7. Consider the places in R. For any $Y_1 \subseteq \Omega_N[r_1]$ such that Y_1 is conflict-free, ${}^{\bullet}r_1 \subseteq T[Y_1] \Rightarrow r_1^{\bullet} \subseteq T[Y_1]$. Similarly, for any $Y_2 \subseteq \Omega_N[r_2]$ such that Y_2 is conflict-free, ${}^{\bullet}r_2 \subseteq T[Y_2] \Rightarrow r_2^{\bullet} \subseteq T[Y_2]$. Both places r_1 and r_2 satisfy the cycle-inclusion property.

The other places, p_1, p_2, p_3, p_4, p_5, p_6, p_7, p_8, p_9 and p_{10}, also satisfy the cycle-inclusion property. For p_1, we have ${}^{\bullet}p_1 = \{ t_8 \}$ and $p_1^{\bullet} = \{ t_2 \}$. For any $Y_1 \subseteq \Omega_N[p_1]$ such that Y_1 is conflict free, $\{ t_8 \} \subseteq T[Y_1] \Rightarrow \{ t_2 \} \subseteq T[Y_1]$. For p_2, we have ${}^{\bullet}p_2 = \{ t_1 \}$ and $p_2^{\bullet} = \{ t_3 \}$. For any $Y_2 \subseteq \Omega_N[p_2]$ such that Y_2 is conflict free, $\{ t_1 \} \subseteq T[Y_2] \Rightarrow \{ t_3 \} \subseteq T[Y_2]$. For p_3, we have ${}^{\bullet}p_3 = \{ t_2 \}$ and $p_3^{\bullet} = \{ t_5 \}$. For any $Y_3 \subseteq \Omega_N[p_3]$ such that Y_3 is conflict free, $\{ t_2 \} \subseteq T[Y_3] \Rightarrow \{ t_5 \} \subseteq T[Y_3]$. The same property applies to p_4, p_5, p_6, p_7, p_8, p_9 and p_{10}.

Example 3.13 Figure 3.9 shows an augmented marked graph $(N, M_0; R)$, where $R = \{ r_1, r_2 \}$. Both r_1 and r_2 do not satisfy the cycle-inclusion property. For r_1, consider $Y_1 = \{ \gamma_{11}, \gamma_{12} \} \subseteq \Omega_N[r_1]$, where $\gamma_{11} = \langle r_1, p_5 \rangle$ and $\gamma_{12} = \langle r_1, p_5, r_2, p_6 \rangle$. Y_1 is conflict free. However, ${}^{\bullet}r_1 = \{ t_5, t_6 \} \subseteq T[Y_1] = \{ t_3, t_4, t_5, t_6 \}$ and $r_1^{\bullet} = \{ t_2, t_3 \} \not\subset T[Y_1]$. Similarly, for r_2, consider $Y_2 = \{ \gamma_{21}, \gamma_{22} \} \subseteq \Omega_N[r_2]$, where $\gamma_{21} = \langle r_2, p_6 \rangle$ and $\gamma_{22} = \langle r_2, p_6, r_1, p_5 \rangle$. Y_2 is conflict free. However, ${}^{\bullet}r_2 = \{ t_5, t_6 \} \subseteq T[Y_2] = \{ t_3, t_4, t_5, t_6 \}$ and $r_2^{\bullet} = \{ t_1, t_4 \} \nsubseteq T[Y_2]$.

On the other hand, those places not in R, including p_1, p_2, p_3, p_4, p_5 and p_6, satisfy the cycle-inclusion property.

Property 3.16 Let $(N, M_0; R)$ an augmented marked graph. $(N, M_0; R)$ satisfies the siphon-trap property, or equivalently, every siphon contains a marked trap if and only if every place of R satisfies the cycle-inclusion property.

Proof ($\Leftarrow$) Let $S = \{ p_1, p_2, \ldots, p_n \}$ be any minimal siphon in N. For each $p_i \in S$, according to Property 3.2, there exists a set of cycles $Y_i \subseteq \Omega_N[p_i]$ such that Y is conflict-free, $P[Y_i] = S$ and ${}^{\bullet}p_i \subseteq T[Y_i]$. Obviously, Y_i is marked, since every cycle in an augmented marked graph is marked according to Property 3.3. Hence, S is marked. According to Property 3.15 and on the assumption that every place $r \in R$ satisfies the cycle-inclusion property, p_i must satisfy the cycle-inclusion property. We have $p_i^{\bullet} \subseteq T[Y_i] = ({}^{\bullet}P[Y_i] \cap P[Y_i]^{\bullet})$, implying $p_i^{\bullet} \subseteq {}^{\bullet}P[Y_i] = {}^{\bullet}S$. Hence, $S^{\bullet} = (p_1^{\bullet} \cup p_2^{\bullet} \cup \ldots \cup p_n^{\bullet}) \subseteq {}^{\bullet}S$, and S is also a marked trap. Hence, every siphon contains itself as a marked trap. ($\Rightarrow$ by contradiction) Suppose there exists a place $r \in R$ not satisfying the cycle-inclusion property. According to Property 3.5, there

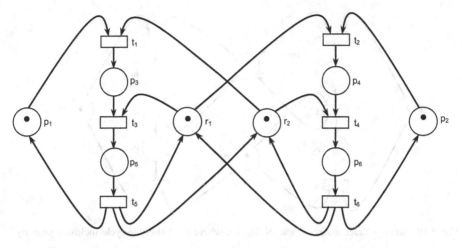

Fig. 3.9 An augmented marked graph for illustration of cycle-inclusion property

exists a siphon S which is marked only by r. There must exist a minimal siphon $S' \subseteq S$. According to Property 3.2, there exists a set of cycles Y such that Y is conflict-free and $P[Y] \subseteq S'$. Obviously, every cycle in Y is marked, since every cycle in an augmented marked graph is marked. Since $S' \subseteq S$ and r is the only one place in S that is marked, r is also the one place in S' that is marked and $Y \subseteq \Omega_N[r]$. Given that every siphon contains a marked trap, let Q be a marked trap in S'. Then, $r \in Q$ and $r^{\bullet} \subseteq (^{\bullet}Q \cap Q^{\bullet})$. Since r does not satisfy the cycle-inclusion property, we have $^{\bullet}r \subseteq T[Y]$ but $r^{\bullet} \nsubseteq T[Y]$. Since S' is a siphon, it is always true for $^{\bullet}r \subseteq (^{\bullet}S' \cap S'^{\bullet}) = (^{\bullet}P[Y] \cap P[Y]^{\bullet}) = T[Y]$. However, since r does not satisfy the cycle-inclusion property, $r^{\bullet} \nsubseteq T[Y] = (^{\bullet}P[Y] \cap P[Y]^{\bullet}) = (^{\bullet}S' \cap S'^{\bullet})$ implies that $r^{\bullet} \nsubseteq (^{\bullet}Q \cap Q^{\bullet})$. $\square$

Property 3.16 essentially shows that an augmented marked graph $(N, M_0; R)$ satisfies the siphon-trap property if and only if every place of R satisfies the cycle-inclusion property. Based on this characterization by the cycle-inclusion property, a sufficient condition of liveness and reversible for augmented marked graphs is derived, as follows.

Property 3.17 An augmented marked graph $(N, M_0; R)$ is live and reversible if it satisfies the siphon-trap property, or equivalently, every place of R satisfies the cycle-inclusion property.

Proof This follows from Properties 3.13 and 3.16. $\square$

Example 3.14 Consider the augmented marked graph $(N, M_0; R)$, where $R = \{ r_1, r_2 \}$, shown in Fig. 3.7. As illustrated in Example 3.11, both r_1 and r_2 satisfy the cycle-inclusion property. Every siphon of $(N, M_0; R)$ contains a marked traps. $(N, M_0; R)$ satisfies the siphon-trap property. $(N, M_0; R)$ is live and reversible.

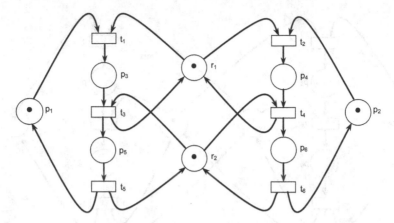

Fig. 3.10 An augmented marked graph $(N, M_0; R)$, where R satisfies the cycle-inclusion property

Example 3.15 Figure 3.10 shows an augmented marked graph $(N, M_0; R)$, where $R = \{ r_1, r_2 \}$. Both r_1 and r_2 satisfy the cycle inclusion property. For any $Y_1 \subseteq \Omega_N[r_1]$ such that Y_1 is conflict-free, ${}^{\bullet}r_1 \subseteq T[Y_1] \Rightarrow r_1{}^{\bullet} \subseteq T[Y_1]$. Similarly, for any $Y_2 \subseteq \Omega_N[r_2]$ such that Y_2 is conflict-free, ${}^{\bullet}r_2 \subseteq T[Y_2] \Rightarrow r_2{}^{\bullet} \subseteq T[Y_2]$. Every siphon of $(N, M_0; R)$ contains a marked traps. $(N, M_0; R)$ satisfies the siphon-trap property. $(N, M_0; R)$ is live and reversible.

Example 3.16 Figure 3.11 shows an augmented marked graph $(N, M_0; R)$, where $R = \{ r_1, r_2 \}$. Both r_1 and r_2 do not satisfy the cycle inclusion property. For r_1, consider $Y_1 = \{ \gamma_{11}, \gamma_{12} \} \subseteq \Omega_N[r_1]$, where $\gamma_{11} = \langle r_1, p_5 \rangle$ and $\gamma_{12} = \langle r_1, p_5, r_2, p_6 \rangle$. Y_1 is conflict free. However, ${}^{\bullet}r_1 = \{ t_5, t_8 \} \subseteq T[Y_1] = \{ t_3, t_4, t_5, t_6 \}$ and $r_1{}^{\bullet} = \{ t_2, t_3 \} \nsubseteq T[Y_1]$. Similarly, for r_2, consider $Y_2 = \{ \gamma_{21}, \gamma_{22} \} \subseteq \Omega_N[r_2]$, where $\gamma_{21} = \langle r_2, p_6 \rangle$ and $\gamma_{22} = \langle r_2, p_6, r_1, p_5 \rangle$. Y_2 is conflict free. However, ${}^{\bullet}r_2 = \{ t_6, t_7 \} \subseteq T[Y_2] = \{ t_3, t_4, t_5, t_6 \}$ and $r_2{}^{\bullet} = \{ t_1, t_4 \} \nsubseteq T[Y_2]$.

   $(N, M_0; R)$ does not satisfy the siphon-trap property. Consider a siphon $S = \{ r_1, r_2, p_5, p_6 \}$. S does not contain any marked trap, and would become empty after firing t_1 and t_2. $(N, M_0; R)$ is neither live nor reversible.

   Based on Properties 3.6, 3.12, 3.14 and 3.17, we derive another strategy for checking the liveness and reversibility of an augmented marked graph, as shown in Algorithm 3.2. The checking starts with checking the cycle-inclusion property for places in R. If all these places satisfy the cycle-inclusion property, then the augmented marked graph is live and reversibility. Otherwise, for those places in R not satisfying the cycle-inclusion property, we check whether each of them contains a marked trap or would eventually become empty.

Algorithm 3.2 Checking the liveness and reversibility of an augmented marked graph $(N, M_0; R)$.

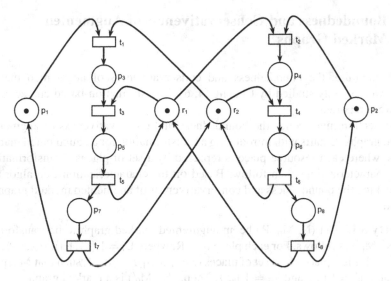

Fig. 3.11 An augmented marked graph $(N, M_0; R)$, where R does not satisfy the cycle-inclusion property

Step 1. Check if every $r \in R$ satisfies the cycle-inclusion property. If yes, report $(N, M_0; R)$ is live and reversible. Otherwise go to Step 2.

Step 2. Let $R' \subseteq R$ be the set of places which do not satisfy the cycle-inclusion property. Based on $\Omega_N[R']$, find all R-siphons which contain at least one place in R'.

Step 3. For each R-siphon identified in Step 2, check if it contains a marked trap. If yes, report $(N, M_0; R)$ is live and reversible. Otherwise, go to Step 4.

Step 4. For each R-siphon identified in Step 2 that does not contain any marked trap, check if it would never become empty. If yes, report $(N, M_0; R)$ is live and reversible. Otherwise, report $(N, M_0; R)$ is neither live nor reversible.

Algorithm 3.2 is more effective than Algorithm 3.1 for checking the liveness and reversibility of an augmented marked graph. Algorithm 3.1 is based on siphons while Algorithm 3.2 is based on cycles.

It is obvious that checking the cycle-inclusion property is simpler than checking the siphon-trap property. The procedure for finding cycles is more straight-forward than finding siphons. Moreover, we only need to consider the fulfilment of cycle-inclusion property for the resource places of an augmented marked graph. This set of resource places is usually small, and thus, a small number of cycles is involved in the checking.

3.4   Boundedness and Conservativeness of Augmented Marked Graphs

In the literature, the boundedness and conservativeness of augmented marked graphs were mainly studied by Cheung [4, 6]. Transformation-based characterizations were reported.

This section investigates the boundedness and conservativeness of augmented marked graphs. It starts with introducing a transformation for an augmented marked graphs, where each resource place is replaced by a set of places. Transformation-based characterizations then follow. Based on the characterizations, an algorithm for checking the boundedness and conservativeness of augmented marked graphs is derived.

Property 3.18 Let $(N, M_0; R)$ be an augmented marked graph to be transformed into (N', M_0') as follows. For each place $r \in R$, where $D_r = \{ \langle t_{s1}, t_{h1} \rangle, \langle t_{s2}, t_{h2} \rangle, \ldots, \langle t_{skr}, t_{hkr} \rangle \}$, r is replaced by a set of places $Q = \{ q_1, q_2, \ldots, q_{kr} \}$, such that $M_0'[p_i] = M_0[r]$ and $q_i^{\bullet} = \{ t_{si} \}$ and $^{\bullet}q_i = \{ t_{hi} \}$. Then, (N', M_0') is a marked graph.

Proof According to the definition of augmented marked graphs, for each place $p \notin R$ in $(N, M_0; R)$, $|^{\bullet}p| = |p^{\bullet}| = 1$. Each place $r \in R$ is replaced by a set of places $Q = \{ q_1, q_2, \ldots, q_{kr} \}$, where $|^{\bullet}q_i| = |q_i^{\bullet}| = 1$ for $i = 1, 2, \ldots, k_r$. Hence, (N', M_0') is a marked graph. $\square$

Definition 3.9 For an augmented marked graph $(N, M_0; R)$, the marked graph (N', M_0') obtained from $(N, M_0; R)$ after the transformation as stated in Property 3.18 is called the R-transform of $(N, M_0; R)$.

Property 3.19 Let (N', M_0') be the R-transform of an augmented marked graph $(N, M_0; R)$. (N', M_0') is a live marked graph.

Proof According to the definition of R-transform, (N', M_0') is a marked graph. The transformation process does not create new cycles. Hence, the cycles in (N', M_0') also exist in $(N, M_0; R)$. According to Property 3.3, every cycle in $(N, M_0; R)$ is marked, and hence, every cycle in (N', M_0') is marked. According to Property 2.7, (N', M_0') is live. $\square$

Example 3.17 Figure 3.12 shows an augmented marked graph $(N, M_0; R)$, and Fig. 3.12 shows the R-transform (N', M_0') of $(N, M_0; R)$, where r is replaced by a set of places $Q = \{ q_1, q_2 \}$. (N', M_0') is a marked graph. Every cycle in (N', M_0') is marked. For example, the cycles $\gamma_1 = \langle p_1, p_4, p_7 \rangle$, $\gamma_2 = \langle q_1, p_5, p_8 \rangle$, $\gamma_3 = \langle p_5, p_8, p_{10}, q_2, p_6, p_3 \rangle$, $\gamma_4 = \langle q_2, p_6, p_3, p_5, p_8, p_{10} \rangle$ and $\gamma_5 = \langle p_2, p_6, p_9 \rangle$ are marked.

Property 3.20 Let $(N, M_0; R)$ be an augmented marked graph, and (N', M_0') be the R-transform of $(N, M_0; R)$, where a place $r \in R$ is replaced by a set of places $Q = \{ q_1, q_2, \ldots, q_k \}$. Then, for each q_i in N', there exists a place invariant α_i of N' such that $\alpha_i[q_i] = 1$ and $\alpha_i[q] = 0$ for any $q \in (P_0 \setminus \{q_i\})$, where P_0 is the set of marked places in (N', M_0').

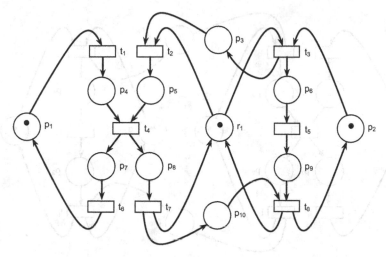

Fig. 3.12 An augmented marked graph $(N, M_0; R)$ for illustration of R-transform

Proof Let $D_r = \{ \langle t_{s1}, t_{h1} \rangle, \langle t_{s2}, t_{h2} \rangle, \ldots, \langle t_{skr}, t_{hkr} \rangle \}$, for $r \in R$. According to the definition of augmented marked graphs, for each $\langle t_{si}, t_{hi} \rangle$, there exists an unmarked path $\rho = \langle t_{s1}, \ldots, t_{h1} \rangle$ in $(N, M_0; R)$. Obviously, ρ also exists as an unmarked path in (N', M_0'), and ρ together with q_i forms a cycle γ_i which is marked at q_i only. As (N', M_0') is a marked graph, according to Property 2.5, the corresponding place vector of γ_i is a place invariant α_i of N'. Since q_i is the only one marked place in γ_i, $\alpha_i[q_i] = 1$ and $\alpha_i[q] = 0$ for any $q \in P_0 \setminus \{q_i\}$. $\square$

Example 3.18 Consider the augmented marked graph $(N, M_0; R)$ shown in Fig. 3.12, and the R-transform (N', M_0') of $(N, M_0; R)$, shown in Fig. 3.13. The place $r_1 \in R$ is replaced by a set of places $Q = \{ q_1, q_2 \}$. $P_0 = \{ q_1, q_2, p_1, p_2 \}$ is the set of marked places in (N', M_0'). α_1 is a place invariant in N', such that $\alpha_1[q_1] = 1$ and $\alpha_1[q_2] = \alpha_1[p_1] = \alpha_1[p_2] = 0$. α_2 is another place invariant in N', such that $\alpha_2[q_2] = 1$, $\alpha_2[q_1] = 0$, $\alpha_2[p_1] = 0$, $\alpha_2[p_2] = 0$.

Property 3.21 Let $(N, M_0; R)$ be an augmented marked graph, where $R = \{ r_1, r_2, \ldots, r_n \}$. Let (N', M_0') be the R-transform of $(N, M_0; R)$, where each r_i is replaced by a set of places Q_i, for $i = 1, 2, \ldots, n$. If every place in (N', M_0') belongs to a cycle, then there exists a place invariant α of N' such that $\alpha > 0$ and $\alpha[q_1] = \alpha[q_2] = \ldots = \alpha[q_k]$ for each $Q_i = \{ q_1, q_2, \ldots, q_k \}$.

Proof Let $P = \{ p_1, p_2, \ldots, p_n \}$ be places in N', and P_0 be those marked places. Since each p_i belongs to a cycle γ_i and (N', M_0') is a marked graph, according to Property 2.5, the corresponding place vector of γ_i is a place invariant α_i'. Then, $\alpha' = \alpha_1' + \alpha_2' + \ldots + \alpha_n' > 0$ is a place invariant. Consider $Q_i = \{ q_1, q_2, \ldots, q_k \}$. Let $q_m \in Q_i$ such that $\alpha'[q_m] \geq \alpha'[q_j]$ for any $q_j \in Q_i$. For each q_j, according to Property 3.20, there exists a place invariant $\alpha_j' > 0$ such that $\alpha_j'[q_j] = 1$ and $\alpha_j'[q] = 0$ for any

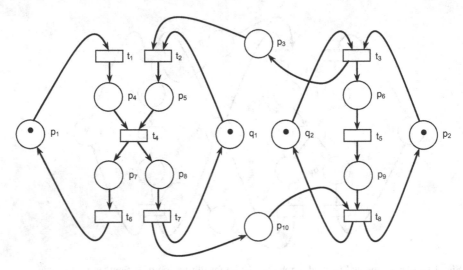

Fig. 3.13 The R-transform (N', M_0') of $(N, M_0; R)$ shown in Fig. 3.12

place $q \in P_0 \backslash \{q_j\}$. There also exists a place invariant $\alpha'' = \alpha' + h\alpha_j'$, where $h \geq$ 1, such that $\alpha''[q_j] = \alpha''[q_m]$ and $\alpha''[s] = \alpha'[q]$ for any $q \in P_0 \backslash \{q_j\}$. Hence, there eventually exists a place invariant α, such that $\alpha[q_1] = \alpha[q_2] = \ldots = \alpha[q_k]$. $\square$

Example 3.19 Consider the augmented marked graph $(N, M_0; R)$, shown in Fig. 3.12, and the R-transform (N', M_0') of $(N, M_0; R)$, shown in Fig. 3.13. The place $r_1 \in R$ is replaced by a set of places $Q = \{ q_1, q_2 \}$. In (N', M_0'), every place belongs to a cycle. α_1 is a place invariant in N', where $\alpha_1[q_1] = 1$ and $\alpha_1[q_2] = 0$. α_2 is another place invariant in N', where $\alpha_2[q_1] = 0$ and $\alpha_2[q_2] = 1$. Then, $\alpha = \alpha_1 + \alpha_2$ is also a place invariant in N', where $\alpha[q_1] = \alpha[q_2] = 1$.

Lemma 3.2 Let $N = \langle P, T, F \rangle$ be a PT-net and $N' = \langle P', T', F' \rangle$ be the PT-net obtained from N after fusing a set of places $Q = \{ q_1, q_2, \ldots, q_n \} \subset P$ into a single place $r \in P'$. If there exists a place invariant α of N such that $\alpha[q_1] = \alpha[q_2] = \ldots = \alpha[q_n] = k \geq 0$, then there also exists a place invariant α' of N' such that $\alpha'[r] = k$ and $\alpha'[s] = \alpha[s]$ for any $s \in P' \backslash \{r\} = P \backslash Q$.

Proof Since N' is obtained from N by fusing $Q = \{ q_1, q_2, \ldots, q_n \}$ into r, we have $P' = (P \backslash Q) \cup \{ r \}$. Let V be the incidence matrix of N. Then, the incidence matrix V' of N' satisfies that $V'[r] = \Sigma_{i=1,2,\ldots,n} V[q_i]$ and $V'[s] = V[s]$ for any $s \in P' \backslash \{r\} = P \backslash Q$. Since α is a place invariant of N, $\alpha V = 0$. Let α' be a place vector of N' such that $\alpha'[r] = \alpha[q_1] = \alpha[q_2] = \ldots = \alpha[q_n] = k$ and $\alpha'[s] = \alpha[s]$ for every $s \in P' \backslash \{r\} = P \backslash Q$. Then, $\alpha'V' = \alpha'[r]V'[r] + \Sigma_{p \in (P' \backslash \{r\})} \alpha'[p]V'[p] = \Sigma_{i=1,2,\ldots,n} \alpha[q_i]V[q_i] + \Sigma_{p \in (P \backslash Q)} \alpha[p]V[p] = \alpha V = 0$. Hence, α' is a place invariant of N'. $\square$

Lemma 3.3 Let $N = \langle P, T, F \rangle$ be a PT-net and $N' = \langle P', T', F' \rangle$ be the PT-net obtained from N after fusing a set of places $Q = \{ q_1, q_2, \ldots, q_n \} \subset P$ into a single place $r \in P'$. If there exists a place invariant α' of N' such that $\alpha'[r] = k \geq 0$, then there also exists a place invariant α of N such that $\alpha[q_1] = \alpha[q_2] = \ldots = \alpha[q_n] = k$ and $\alpha[s] = \alpha'[s]$ for any $s \in P\backslash Q = P'\backslash\{r\}$.

Proof Since N' is obtained from N by fusing $Q = \{ q_1, q_2, \ldots, q_n \}$ into r, we have $P' = (P\backslash Q) \cup \{ r \}$. Let V be the incidence matrix of N. Then, the incidence matrix V' of N' satisfies that $V'[r] = \Sigma_{i=1,2,\ldots,n} V[q_i]$ and $V'[s] = V[s]$ for any $s \in P'\backslash\{r\} = P\backslash Q$. Since α' is a place invariant of N', $\alpha'V' = 0$. Let α be a place vector of N such that $\alpha[q_1] = \alpha[q_2] = \ldots = \alpha[q_n] = k$ and $\alpha[s] = \alpha'[s]$ for every $s \in P\backslash Q = P'\backslash\{r\}$. Then, $\alpha V = \Sigma_{i=1,2,\ldots,n}\alpha[q_i]V[q_i] + \Sigma_{p \in (P\backslash Q)}\alpha[p]V[p] = \alpha'[r]V'[r] + \Sigma_{p \in (P'\backslash\{r\})}\alpha'[p]V'[p] = \alpha'V'$. Hence, α is a place invariant of N. $\square$

In the following, a necessary and sufficient condition for the boundedness and conservativeness for augmented marked graphs is derived.

Property 3.22 Let $(N, M_0; R)$ be an augmented marked graph, and (N', M_0') be the R-transform of $(N, M_0; R)$. $(N, M_0; R)$ is bounded and conservative if and only if every place in (N', M_0') belongs to a cycle.

Proof Let (N', M_0') be the R-transform of $(N, M_0; R)$, where each r_i is replaced by a set of places Q_i, for $i = 1, 2, \ldots, n$. ($\Leftarrow$) Since every place in (N', M_0') belongs to a cycle, according to Property 3.20, there exists a place invariant α' of N' such that $\alpha' > 0$ and $\alpha'[q_1] = \alpha'[q_2] = \ldots = \alpha'[q_k]$ for each $Q_i = \{ q_1, q_2, \ldots, q_k \}$. It follows from Lemma 3.2 that there also exists a place invariants α of N such that $\alpha > 0$ and $\alpha[r_i] = \alpha'[q_1] = \alpha'[q_2] = \ldots = \alpha'[q_k]$ for each Q_i. Hence, $(N, M_0; R)$ is conservative. It follows from Property 2.2 that $(N, M_0; R)$ is bounded. ($\Rightarrow$) Given that $(N, M_0; R)$ is bounded and conservative, there exists a place invariant α of N such that $\alpha > 0$. Consider each $r_i \in R$ which is replaced by $Q_i = \{ q_1, q_2, \ldots, q_k \}$. According to Lemma 3.3, there also exists a place invariant α' of N' such that $\alpha' > 0$ and $\alpha'[q_1] = \alpha'[q_2] = \ldots = \alpha'[q_k] = \alpha[r_i]$ and $\alpha'[s] = \alpha[s]$ for any $s \in P\backslash Q_i$. It follows from Property 2.2 that (N', M_0') is bounded. According to Properties 3.19, (N', M_0') is a live marked graph. It then follows from 2.7 that every place in (N', M_0') belongs to a cycle. $\square$

According to Property 3.19, the R-transform (N', M_0') of an augmented marked graph $(N, M_0; R)$ is a live marked graph. In case every place in (N', M_0') belongs to a cycle, according to Property 2.8, (N', M_0') is indeed a live and bounded marked graph. It follows from Property 3.22 that $(N, M_0; R)$ is bounded and conservative if and only if (N', M_0') is live and bounded.

Example 3.20 Consider the augmented marked graph $(N, M_0; R)$, shown in Fig. 3.12, and the R-transform (N', M_0') of $(N, M_0; R)$, shown in Fig. 3.13. Every place in (N', M_0') belongs to a cycle. For example, p_1 belongs to $\gamma_1 = \langle p_1, p_4, p_7 \rangle \in \Omega_{N'}$, p_2 belongs to $\gamma_2 = \langle p_2, p_6, p_9 \rangle \in \Omega_{N'}$, and p_3 belongs to $\gamma_3 = \langle p_3, p_5, p_8, p_{10}, p_9, p_6 \rangle \in \Omega_{N'}$. (N', M_0') is a live and bounded marked graph. $(N, M_0; R)$ is bounded and conservative.

Example 3.21 Figure 3.14 shows another augmented marked graph $(N, M_0; R)$. Figure 3.15 shows the R-transform (N', M_0') of $(N, M_0; R)$, where r is replaced by

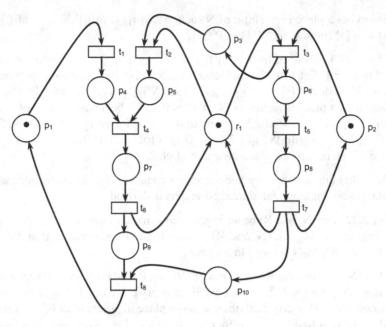

Fig. 3.14 Another augmented marked graph (N, M₀; R) for illustration of R-transform

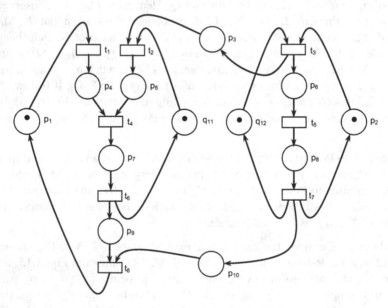

Fig. 3.15 The R-transform (N′, M₀′) of (N, M₀; R) shown in Fig. 3.14

{ q_1, q_2 }. For (N', M_0'), some places do not belong to any cycle. As, for example, p_3 and p_{10} do not belong to any cycle in (N', M_0'). $(N, M_0; R)$ is neither bounded nor conservative. At the initial marking M_0, where $M_0(p_1) = M_0(p_2) = M_0(r_1) = 1$ and $M_0(p_3) = M_0(p_4) = M_0(p_5) = M_0(p_6) = M_0(p_7) = M_0(p_8) = M_0(p_9) = M_0(p_{10}) = 0$, if repeatedly firing t_3, t_5 and t_7, then p_3 and p_{10} would accumulate more and more tokens, and become unbounded.

Based on Properties 3.22, we derive a strategy for checking the boundedness and conservativeness of an augmented marked graph, as shown in Algorithm 3.3. The checking starts with identifying cycles in the R-transform of the augmented marked graph. If every place in the R-transform belongs to a cycle, then the augmented marked graph is bounded and conservative.

Algorithm 3.3 Checking the boundedness and conservativeness of an augmented marked graph $(N, M_0; R)$.

Step 1.   Create the R-transform (N', M_0') of $(N, M_0; R)$.
Step 2.   Find the set of cycles $\Omega_{N'}$ in N'.
Step 3.   For each place p in (N', M_0'), check if there exists a cycle $\gamma \in \Omega_{N'}$ such that $p \in P[\gamma]$. If yes, report that $(N, M_0; R)$ is bounded and conservative. Otherwise, report that $(N, M_0; R)$ is neither bounded nor conservative.

References

1. F. Chu, X. Xie, Deadlock analysis of Petri nets using siphons and mathematical programming. IEEE Trans. Robot. Autom. **13**(6), 793–804 (1997)
2. K.S. Cheung, New characterisation for live and reversible augmented marked graphs. Inf. Process. Lett. **92**(5), 239–243 (2004)
3. K.S. Cheung, K.O. Chow, Cycle-inclusion property of augmented marked graphs. Inf. Process. Lett. **94**(6), 271–276 (2005)
4. K.S. Cheung, Augmented marked graphs. Informatica **32**(1), 85–94 (2008)
5. K. Barkaoui et al., On liveness in extended non self-controlling net, in *Application and Theory of Petri Nets*, ed. by G.D. Michelis, M. Diaz. Lecture Notes in Computer Science, vol. 935 (Springer, Berlin, 1995), pp. 25–44
6. K.S. Cheung, Boundedness and conservativeness of augmented marked graphs. IMA J. Math. Control. Inf. **24**(2), 235–24 (2007)

Chapter 4
Proper Augmented Marked Graphs

A special type of augmented marked graphs, proper augmented marked graphs, not only inherit the properties of augmented marked graphs but also possess some special properties. This chapter provides a comprehensive description of proper augmented marked graphs. It starts with the definition of proper augmented marked graphs. A detailed analysis of the special properties of proper augmented marked graphs then follows.

4.1 Definition and Terminology

Let us revisit the definition of augmented marked graphs [1–3]. In an augmented marked graph $(N, M_0; R)$, for each $r \in R$, there exist $k_r > 1$ pairs of transitions $D_r = \{ \langle t_{s1}, t_{h1} \rangle, \langle t_{s2}, t_{h2} \rangle, \ldots, \langle t_{skr}, t_{hkr} \rangle \}$, such that $r^\bullet = \{ t_{s1}, t_{s2}, \ldots, t_{skr} \}$ and $^\bullet r = \{ t_{h1}, t_{h2}, \ldots, t_{hkr} \}$, and hence, $| ^\bullet r | = | r^\bullet | > 1$. Consider a variation that also allows the existence of only one pair of transitions $D_r = \{ \langle t_s, t_h \rangle \}$ for r. Then, for each $r \in R$, $| ^\bullet r | = | r^\bullet | \geq 1$. We introduce a special type of augmented marked graphs called proper augmented marked graphs, which allows this variation while satisfying one further condition that every place in the R-transform belongs to a cycle.

Definition 4.1 Let $(N, M_0; R)$ be an augmented marked graph, and (N', M_0') be the R-transform of $(N, M_0; R)$. $(N, M_0; R)$ is a proper augmented marked graph if and only if : (a) For each $r \in R$, $| ^\bullet r | = | r^\bullet | \geq 1$. (b) Every place in (N', M_0') belongs to a cycle.

Example 4.1 Figure 4.1 shows an augmented marked graph $(N, M_0; R)$, where $R = \{r_1, r_2\}$. Figure 4.2 shows the R-transform (N', M_0') of $(N, M_0; R)$, where each place belongs to a cycle. $(N, M_0; R)$ is a proper augmented marked graph.

Example 4.2 Figure 4.3 shows an augmented marked graph $(N, M_0; R)$, where $R = \{r_1, r_2\}$. Figure 4.4 shows the R-transform (N', M_0') of $(N, M_0; R)$, where p_3 and p_8

K.S. Cheung, *Augmented Marked Graphs*, DOI 10.1007/978-3-319-06428-4_4,

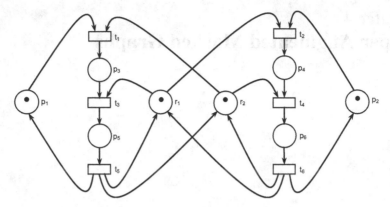

Fig. 4.1 A proper augmented marked graph $(N, M_0; R)$

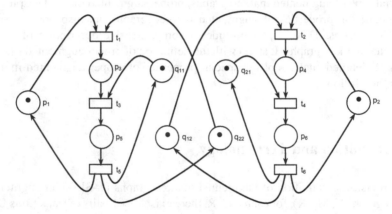

Fig. 4.2 The R-transform (N', M_0') of $(N, M_0; R)$ shown in Fig. 4.1

do not belong to any cycle. Hence, $(N, M_0; R)$ is not a proper augmented marked graph.

Example 4.3 Figure 4.5 shows a proper augmented marked graph $(N, M_0; R)$, where $R = \{r_1, r_2\}$. Figure 4.6 shows the R-transform (N', M_0') of $(N, M_0; R)$, where every place belongs to a cycle. For $r_2 \in R$, there exists one pair of transitions $D_{r_2} = \{\langle t_3, t_8 \rangle\}$ such that $r_2{}^\bullet = \{t_3\}$ and ${}^\bullet r_2 = \{t_8\}$. This is the slight variation from the definition of augmented marked graphs, as stated in Definition 3.1.

4.2 Properties of Proper Augmented Marked Graphs

A proper augmented marked graph is structurally an augmented marked graph, and possesses all the properties described in Chap. 3. This section focus on the special properties of proper augmented marked graphs.

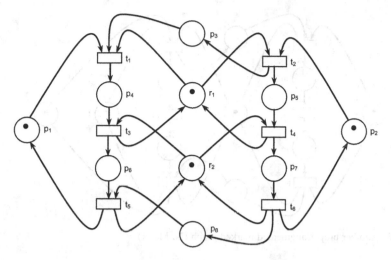

Fig. 4.3 An augmented marked graph $(N, M_0; R)$ which is not a proper augmented marked graph

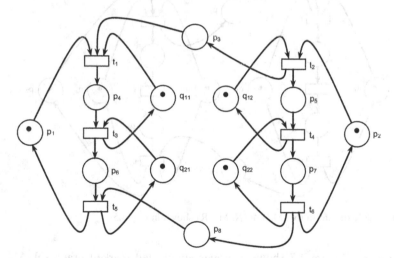

Fig. 4.4 The R-transform (N', M_0') of $(N, M_0; R)$ shown in Fig. 4.3

Property 4.1 A proper augmented marked graph $(N, M_0; R)$ is structurally a live, bounded and conservative marked graph if and only if, $\forall r \in R, |\,^\bullet r\,| = |\, r^\bullet\,| = 1$.

Proof ($\Leftarrow$) It is obvious that $(N, M_0; R)$ is a marked graph, where every place belongs to a cycle and every cycle is marked. According to Properties 2.6, 2.7 and 2.8, $(N, M_0; R)$ is live, bounded and conservative. ($\Rightarrow$) Since $(N, M_0; R)$ is a marked graph, the condition $|\,^\bullet r\,| = |\, r^\bullet\,| = 1$ should always hold for every $r \in R$. $\square$

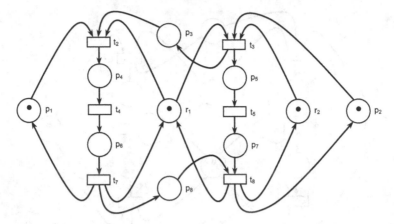

Fig. 4.5 Another proper augmented marked graph (N, M₀; R)

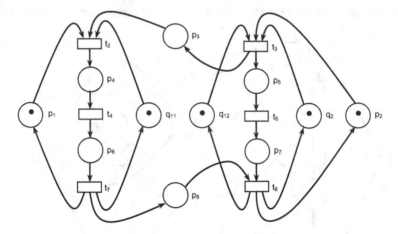

Fig. 4.6 The R-transform (N′, M₀′) of (N, M₀; R) shown in Fig. 4.5

Example 4.4 Figure 4.7 shows a proper augmented marked graph $(N, M_0; R)$, where $R = \{r_1, r_2\}$. We have $|\,{}^\bullet r_1\,| = |\,r_1{}^\bullet\,| = 1$ and $|\,{}^\bullet r_2\,| = |\,r_2{}^\bullet\,| = 1$. $(N, M_0; R)$ is structurally a live, bounded and conservative marked graph.

Property 4.2 A proper augmented marked graph $(N, M_0; R)$ is structurally an augmented marked graph unless $\forall\, r \in R, |\,{}^\bullet r\,| = |\,r{}^\bullet\,| = 1$.

Proof Let $R' \subseteq R$, where $\forall\, r' \in R', |\,{}^\bullet r'\,| = |\,r'{}^\bullet\,| > 1$. Consider $(N, M_0; R')$. The PT-net (N', M_0') obtained from $(N, M_0; R)$ by removing the places in R and their associated arcs is a marked graph. For (N', M_0'), every cycle is marked. Obviously, $(N, M_0; R')$ is an augmented marked graph. Hence, $(N, M_0; R)$ is structurally an augmented marked graph. □

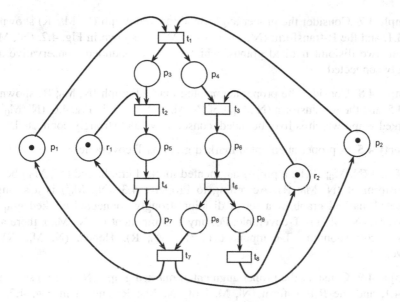

Fig. 4.7 A proper augmented marked graph which is also a live, bounded and conservative marked graph

Example 4.5 Consider the proper augmented marked graph $(N, M_0; R)$, where $R = \{r_1, r_2\}$, shown in Fig. 4.5. For $r_1 \in R$, $|{}^\bullet r_1| = |r_1{}^\bullet| = 2$. Let $R' = \{r_1\}$. $(N, M_0; R')$ is an augmented marked graph. $(N, M_0; R)$ is structurally an augmented marked graph.

Property 4.3 A proper augmented marked graph is bounded and conservative.

Proof Let $(N, M_0; R)$ be a proper augmented marked graph, and (N', M_0') be the R-transform of $(N, M_0; R)$. According to the definition of a proper augmented marked graph, (N', M_0') is a marked graph or a set of marked graphs, where each cycle is marked and every place belongs to a cycle. It follows from Property 3.22 that $(N, M_0; R)$ is bounded and conservative. □

Example 4.6 Consider the proper augmented marked graph $(N, M_0; R)$ shown in Fig. 4.5, and the R-transform (N', M_0') of $(N, M_0; R)$ shown in Fig. 4.6. In (N, M_0'), every place belongs to a cycle. $(N, M_0; R)$ is bounded and conservative.

Property 4.4 Let $(N, M_0; R)$ be a proper augmented marked graph, and (N', M_0') be the R-transform of $(N, M_0; R)$. (N', M_0') is a marked graph which is live, bounded, conservative and strongly connected, or a set of disjoint marked graphs which are live, bounded, conservative and strongly connected.

Proof According to the definition of a proper augmented marked graph, (N', M_0') is a marked graph or a set of marked graphs, where each cycle is marked and every place belongs to a cycle. It follows from Properties 2.6, 2.7, 2.8 and 2.9 that (N', M_0') is live, bounded, conservative and strongly connected. □

Example 4.7 Consider the proper augmented marked graph $(N, M_0; R)$ shown in Fig. 4.1, and the R-transform (N', M_0') of $(N, M_0; R)$ shown in Fig. 4.2. (N', M_0') contains two disjoint marked graphs, which are live, bounded, conservative and strongly connected.

Example 4.8 Consider the proper augmented marked graph $(N, M_0; R)$ shown in Fig. 4.5, and the R-transform (N', M_0') of $(N, M_0; R)$ shown in Fig. 4.6. (N', M_0') is a marked graph which is live, bounded, conservative and strongly connected.

Property 4.5 A proper augmented marked graph is T-coverable.

Proof Let $(N, M_0; R)$ be a proper augmented marked graph, and (N', M_0') be the R-transform of $(N, M_0; R)$. According to Property 4.3, (N', M_0') is a strongly connected marked graph or a set of disjoint strongly connected marked graphs. Obviously, (N', M_0') is T-coverable. For any T-component in (N', M_0'), there also exists a corresponding T-component in $(N, M_0; R)$. Hence, $(N, M_0; R)$ is T-coverable. □

Example 4.9 Consider the proper augmented marked graph $(N, M_0; R)$ shown in Fig. 4.1, and the R-transform (N', M_0') of $(N, M_0; R)$ shown in Fig. 4.2. As illustrated in Example 4.7, (N', M_0') contains two disjoint strongly connected marked graphs. They are T-components of (N', M_0'). There also exists corresponding T-components in $(N, M_0; R)$. $(N, M_0; R)$ is T-coverable.

Example 4.10 Consider the proper augmented marked graph $(N, M_0; R)$ shown in Fig. 4.5, and the R-transform (N', M_0') of $(N, M_0; R)$ shown in Fig. 4.6. As illustrated in Example 4.8, (N', M_0') is a strongly connected marked graph. Obviously, (N', M_0') is T-coverable. For any T-component in (N', M_0'), there also exists a corresponding T-component in $(N, M_0; R)$. Figure 4.8 shows the T-components of $(N, M_0; R)$. $(N, M_0; R)$ is T-coverable.

Property 4.6 Let $(N, M_0; R)$ be a proper augmented marked graph, and (N', M_0') be the R-transform of $(N, M_0; R)$. For any $\gamma \in \Omega_{N'}$, there exists $Y \subseteq \Omega_{N'}$, such that $\gamma \in Y$ and $T[Y] = {}^\bullet P[Y] \cup P[Y]^\bullet$.

Proof Let $R = \{r_1, r_2, \ldots, r_n\}$, where each r_i is replaced by a set of places Q_i in (N', M_0'), for $i = 1, 2, \ldots, n$. In case $\gamma \in \Omega_{N'}[Q_i]$, for any $i = 1, 2, \ldots, n$, there exists $Y \subseteq \Omega_{N'}[Q_i]$, such that $T[Y] = {}^\bullet P[Y] \cup P[Y]^\bullet$. In case $\gamma \notin \Omega_{N'}[Q_i]$, we have $T[\gamma] = {}^\bullet P[\gamma] \cup P[\gamma]^\bullet$. □

Example 4.11 Figure 4.9 shows a proper augmented marked graph $(N, M_0; R)$. Figure 4.10 shows the R-transform (N', M_0') of $(N, M_0; R)$, where r_1 is replaced by $Q_1 = \{q_{11}, q_{12}\}$, and r_2 by $Q_2 = \{q_{21}, q_{22}\}$. Consider $\gamma = \langle p_1, p_3, p_5 \rangle \notin \Omega_{N'}[Q_i]$, for $i = 1, 2$. We have $T[\gamma] = {}^\bullet P[\gamma] \cup P[\gamma]^\bullet$. Consider $\gamma_1 = \langle p_2, p_3, p_5, p_7, q_{22}, q_{12} \rangle \in \Omega_{N'}[Q_i]$, for $i = 1, 2$. There exists $Y = \{\gamma_1, \gamma_2, \gamma_3\} \subseteq \Omega_{N'}[Q_i]$, where $\gamma_2 = \langle p_3, q_{11} \rangle$ and $\gamma_3 = \langle p_5, q_{21} \rangle$. We have $P[Y] = \{p_2, p_3, p_5, p_7, q_{11}, q_{12}, q_{21}, q_{22}\}$ and $T[Y] = {}^\bullet P[Y] \cup P[Y]^\bullet = \{t_1, t_2, t_3, t_4, t_5, t_6\}$.

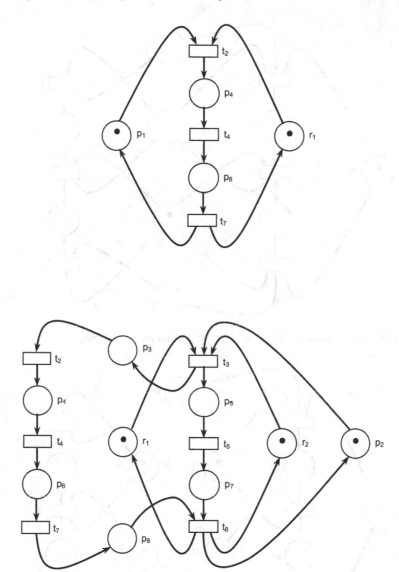

Fig. 4.8 The T-components of $(N, M_0; R)$ shown in Fig. 4.5

Property 4.7 Let $(N, M_0; R)$ be a proper augmented marked graph. For any place p in $(N, M_0; R)$, there exists a set of cycles $Y \subseteq \Omega_N$, such that $p \in P[Y]$ and $T[Y] = {}^{\bullet}P[Y] \cup P[Y]^{\bullet}$.

Proof There are two possible cases for a place p in $(N, M_0; R)$. Consider the case, where p is a place $r \in R$. There exist $k_r \geq 1$ pairs of transitions $D_r = \{ \langle t_{s1}, t_{h1} \rangle, \langle t_{s2}, t_{h2} \rangle, \ldots, \langle t_{skr}, t_{hkr} \rangle \}$, such that each t_{si} connects to t_{hi} via an elementary path ρ_{ri}. Each

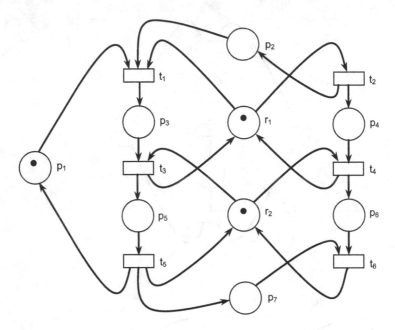

Fig. 4.9 A proper augmented marked graph $(N, M_0; R)$ for illustration of cycles

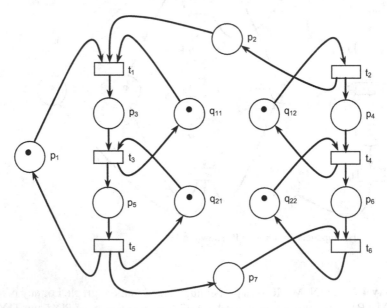

Fig. 4.10 The R-transform (N', M_0') of $(N, M_0; R)$ shown in Fig. 4.9

ρ_i together with r form a cycle $\gamma_i \in \Omega_N[r]$. We have $Y = \{\gamma_1, \gamma_2, \ldots, \gamma_{kr}\} \subseteq \Omega_N[r]$, such that $T[Y] = {}^{\bullet}P[Y] \cup P[Y]^{\bullet}$. Consider the case, where $p \notin R$. It is obvious that p also exists in the R-transform (N', M_0') of $(N, M_0; R)$. Hence, p belongs to a cycle γ in (N', M_0'). It follows from Property 4.6 that there exists $Y' \subseteq \Omega_{N'}$, such that $\gamma \in Y'$ and $T[Y'] = {}^{\bullet}P[Y'] \cup P[Y']^{\bullet}$. There also exists $Y \subseteq \Omega_N$, corresponding to $Y' \subseteq \Omega_{N'}$, such that $T[Y] = {}^{\bullet}P[Y] \cup P[Y]^{\bullet}$. $\square$

Example 4.12 Consider the proper augmented marked graph $(N, M_0; R)$ shown in Fig. 4.9. For any place p in $(N, M_0; R)$, there exists $Y \subseteq \Omega_N$, such that $p \in P[Y]$ and $T[Y] = {}^{\bullet}P[Y] \cup P[Y]^{\bullet}$.

Consider the case, where p is a place in R. For $r_1 \in R$, there exists $Y_1 = \{\gamma_{11}, \gamma_{12}\} \subseteq \Omega_N$, where $\gamma_{11} = \langle r_1, p_3 \rangle$ and $\gamma_{12} = \langle r_1, p_4 \rangle$. We have $r_1 \in P[Y_1] = \{r_1, p_3, p_4\}$ and $T[Y_1] = {}^{\bullet}P[Y_1] \cup P[Y_1]^{\bullet} = \{t_1, t_2, t_3, t_4\}$. Similarly, for $r_2 \in R$, there exists $Y_2 = \{\gamma_{21}, \gamma_{22}\} \subseteq \Omega_N$, where $\gamma_{21} = \langle r_2, p_5 \rangle$ and $\gamma_{22} = \langle r_2, p_6 \rangle$. We have $r_2 \in P[Y_2] = \{r_2, p_5, p_6\}$ and $T[Y_2] = {}^{\bullet}P[Y_2] \cup P[Y_2]^{\bullet} = \{t_3, t_4, t_5, t_6\}$.

Consider the case, where p is not a place in R. Let us use p_1, p_2 and p_3 for illustration. For $p_1 \notin R$, there exists $Y_3 = \{\gamma_{31}\} \subseteq \Omega_N$, where $\gamma_{31} = \langle p_1, p_3, p_5 \rangle$. We have $p_1 \in P[Y_3] = \{p_1, p_3, p_5\}$ and $T[Y_3] = {}^{\bullet}P[Y_3] \cup P[Y_3]^{\bullet} = \{t_1, t_3, t_5\}$. For $p_2 \notin R$, there exists $Y_4 = \{\gamma_{41}, \gamma_{42}, \gamma_{43}\} \subseteq \Omega_N$, where $\gamma_{41} = \langle p_2, p_3, p_5, p_7, p_6, p_4 \rangle$, $\gamma_{42} = \langle r_1, p_3 \rangle$ and $\gamma_{43} = \langle r_2, p_5 \rangle$. We have $p_2 \in P[Y_4] = \{p_2, p_3, p_4, p_5, p_6, p_7, r_1, r_2\}$ and $T[Y_4] = {}^{\bullet}P[Y_4] \cup P[Y_4]^{\bullet} = \{t_1, t_2, t_3, t_4, t_5, t_6\}$. Similarly, for $p_3 \notin R$, there exists $Y_5 = \{\gamma_{51}\} \subseteq \Omega_N$, where $\gamma_{51} = \langle p_1, p_3, p_5 \rangle$. We have $p_3 \in P[Y_5] = \{p_1, p_3, p_5\}$ and $T[Y_5] = {}^{\bullet}P[Y_5] \cup P[Y_5]^{\bullet} = \{t_1, t_3, t_5\}$. The same property applies to other places, p_4, p_5, p_6 and p_7.

Property 4.8 A proper augmented marked graph is P-coverable.

Proof Let $(N, M_0; R)$ be a proper augmented marked graph. For any place p in $(N, M_0; R)$, according to Property 4.7, there exists $Y \subseteq \Omega_N$, such that $p \in P[Y]$ and $T[Y] = {}^{\bullet}P[Y] \cup P[Y]^{\bullet}$. Let $S = \langle P_S, T_S, F_S \rangle$ be a subnet of $(N, M_0; R)$, where $P_S = P[Y]$ and $T_S = T[Y]$. Since $T_S = {}^{\bullet}P_S \cup P_S^{\bullet}$ and, for any $t \in T_S$, $|{}^{\bullet}t| = |t^{\bullet}| = 1$, S is P-component of $(N, M_0; R)$. Hence, p belongs to a P-component. Since all places in $(N, M_0; R)$ belongs to a P-component, $(N, M_0; R)$ is covered by P-components. $(N, M_0; R)$ is P-coverable. $\square$

Example 4.13 Consider the proper augmented marked graph $(N, M_0; R)$ shown in Fig. 4.9. Figure 4.11 shows the P-components of $(N, M_0; R)$. $(N, M_0; R)$ is P-coverable.

Property 4.9 A proper augmented marked graph is both P-coverable and T-coverable.

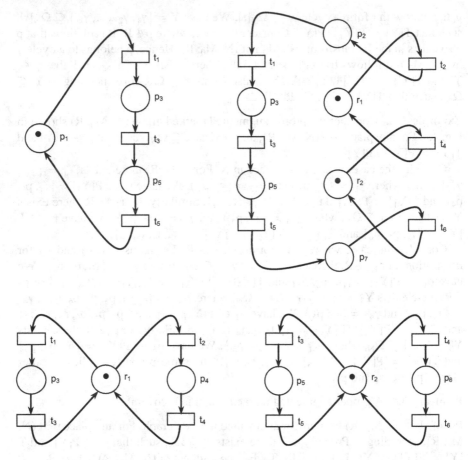

Fig. 4.11 The P-components of (N, M_0; R) shown in Fig. 4.9

Proof It simply follows from Properties 4.5 and 4.8. □

Example 4.14 Consider the proper augmented marked graph (N, M_0; R) shown in Fig. 4.9. As illustrated in Example 4.11, (N, M_0; R) is P-coverable. Figure 4.12 shows the T-components of (N, M_0; R). (N, M_0; R) is also T-coverable.

Fig. 4.12 The
T-components of $(N, M_0; R)$
shown in Fig. 4.9

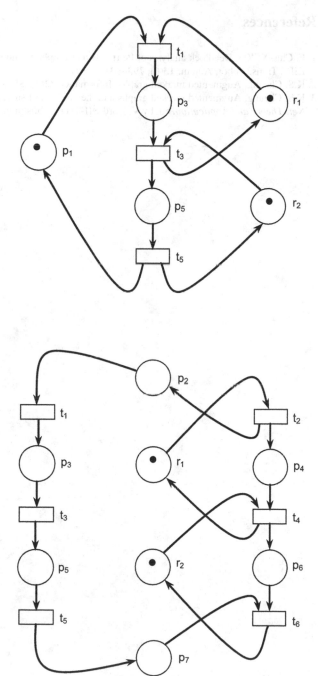

References

1. F. Chu, X. Xie, Deadlock analysis of Petri nets using siphons and mathematical programming. IEEE Trans. Robot. Autom. **13**(6), 793–804 (1997)
2. K.S. Cheung, Augmented marked graphs. Informatica **32**(1), 85–94 (2008)
3. K.S. Cheung, Augmented marked graphs and the analysis of shared resource systems, in *Petri Net: Theory and Application*, ed. by V. Kordic (I-Tech Publishing, Vienna, 2008), pp. 377–400

Chapter 5
Composition of Augmented Marked Graphs

This chapter investigates the composition of augmented marked graphs with a special focus on the preservation of properties. It starts with defining the composition of two augmented marked graphs via common resource places. We show that the integrated PT-net so obtained is also an augmented marked graph. A detailed analysis on the preservation of liveness, reversibility, boundedness and conservativeness for this composition then follows.

5.1 Composition via Common Resource Places

Let us consider two augmented marked graphs $(N_1, M_{10}; R_1)$ and $(N_2, M_{20}; R_2)$. Suppose that $r_{11} \in R_1$ and $r_{21} \in R_2$ refer to the same common resource. Then, r_{11} and r_{21} are called common resource places in $(N_1, M_{10}; R_1)$ and $(N_2, M_{20}; R_2)$. Suppose there also exist another two common resource places $r_{12} \in R_1$ and $r_{22} \in R_2$. Then, $(N_1, M_{10}; R_1)$ and $(N_2, M_{20}; R_2)$ are composed via their common resource places, in the sense that r_{11} and r_{21} are fused into one resource place r_1, and r_{12} and r_{22} into r_2. The resulting PT-net obtained is also an augmented marked graph, as depicted in the following property.

Property 5.1 Let $(N_1, M_{10}; R_1)$ and $(N_2, M_{20}; R_2)$ be two augmented marked graphs. $R_1' = \{r_{11}, r_{12}, \ldots, r_{1k}\} \subseteq R_1$ and $R_2' = \{r_{21}, r_{22}, \ldots, r_{2k}\} \subseteq R_2$ are the common resource places, where $M_{10}(R_1') = M_{20}(R_2')$. Suppose that r_{11} and r_{21} are to be fused into one single place r_1, r_{12} and r_{22} into r_2, ..., r_{1k} and r_{2k} into r_k. Then, the resulting PT-net so obtained is also an augmented marked graph $(N, M_0; R)$, where $R = (R_1 \backslash R_1') \cup (R_2 \backslash R_2') \cup \{r_1, r_2, \ldots, r_k\}$. (obvious)

Example 5.1 Figure 5.1 shows two augmented marked graphs $(N_1, M_{10}; R_1)$ and $(N_2, M_{20}; R_2)$, where $r_{11} \in R_1$ and $r_{21} \in R_2$ refer to the same common resource, and are to be fused. Figure 5.2 shows the integrated augmented marked graph $(N, M_0; R)$, obtained by composing $(N_1, M_{10}; R_1)$ and $(N_2, M_{20}; R_2)$ via their common resource places. For $(N, M_0; R)$, $r_1 \in R$ is the fused place of r_{11} and r_{21}.

K.S. Cheung, *Augmented Marked Graphs*, DOI 10.1007/978-3-319-06428-4_5,
© Springer International Publishing Switzerland 2014

Fig. 5.1 Augmented
marked graphs (N_1, M_{10}, R_1) and (N_2, M_{20}, R_2) with
common resource places

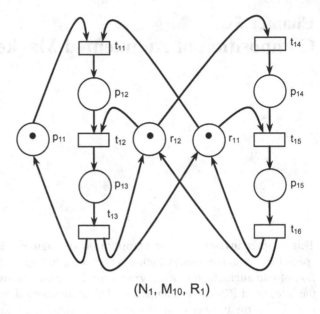

(N_1, M_{10}, R_1)

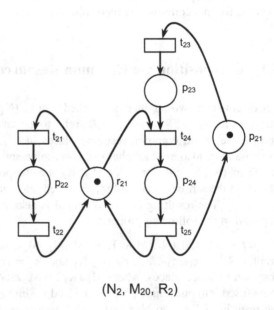

(N_2, M_{20}, R_2)

The composition of two augmented marked graphs is now formally defined as follows.

Definition 5.1 Let $(N_1, M_{10}; R_1)$ and $(N_2, M_{20}; R_2)$ be two augmented marked graphs, to be composed via a set of common resource places $\{(r_{11}, r_{21}), (r_{12}, r_{22}), \ldots, (r_{1k}, r_{2k})\}$, where $r_{11}, r_{12}, \ldots, r_{1k} \in R_1$ and $r_{21}, r_{22}, \ldots, r_{2k} \in R_2$, and $M_{10}(r_{11},$

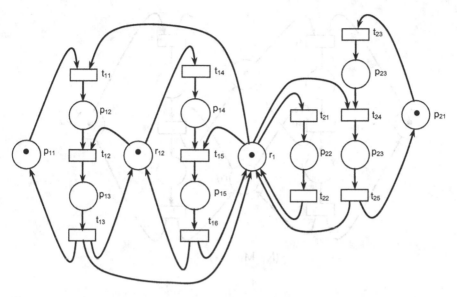

Fig. 5.2 The integrated augmented marked graph obtained by composing the augmented marked graphs in Fig. 5.1

$r_{12}, \ldots, r_{1k}) = M_{20}(r_{21}, r_{22}, \ldots, r_{2k})$. According to Property 5.1, the PT-net so obtained is also an augmented marked graph $(N, M_0; R)$. $(N, M_0; R)$ is called the integrated augmented marked graph.

Example 5.2 Figure 5.3 shows three augmented marked graphs, $(N_1, M_{10}; R_1)$, $(N_2, M_{20}; R_2)$ and $(N_3, M_{30}; R_3)$, where $r_{11} \in R_1$ in $(N_1, M_{10}; R_1)$ and $r_{21} \in R_2$ in $(N_2, M_{20}; R_2)$ refer to the same common resource. Besides, $r_{12} \in R_1$ in $(N_1, M_{10}; R_1)$ and $r_{32} \in R_3$ in $(N_3, M_{30}; R_3)$ refer to the same common resource. Figure 5.4 shows the integrated augmented marked graph $(N', M_0'; R')$ obtained by composing $(N_1, M_{10}; R_1)$ and $(N_2, M_{20}; R_2)$ via their common resource places, where r_{11} and r_{21} are fused into one resource place r_1. Figure 5.5 shows the integrated augmented marked graph $(N, M_0; R)$ obtained by composing $(N', M_0'; R')$ and $(N_3, M_{30}; R_3)$ via their common resource places, where r_{12} and r_{32} are fused into one resource place r_2.

Property 5.2 The integrated augmented marked graph obtained by composing two proper augmented marked graphs via their common resource places is also a proper augmented marked graph.

Proof Let $(N_1, M_{10}; R_1)$ and $(N_2, M_{20}; R_2)$ be two proper augmented marked graph, and $(N, M_0; R)$ be the integrated augmented marked graph obtained by composing $(N_1, M_{10}; R_1)$ and $(N_2, M_{20}; R_2)$ via their common resource places. Let (N_1', M_{10}'), (N_2', M_{20}') and (N', M_0') be the R-transforms of $(N_1, M_{10}; R_1)$, $(N_2, M_{20}; R_2)$ and $(N, M_0; R)$, respectively. Since $(N_1, M_{10}; R_1)$ and $(N_2, M_{20}; R_2)$ are proper augmented marked graphs, every place in (N_1', M_{10}') belongs to a cycle, and

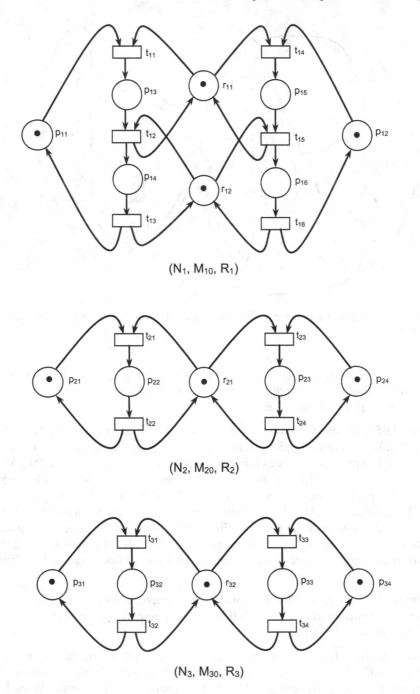

(N_1, M_{10}, R_1)

(N_2, M_{20}, R_2)

(N_3, M_{30}, R_3)

Fig. 5.3 Augmented marked graphs (N_1, M_{10}, R_1), (N_2, M_{20}, R_2) and (N_3, M_{30}, R_3) with common resource places

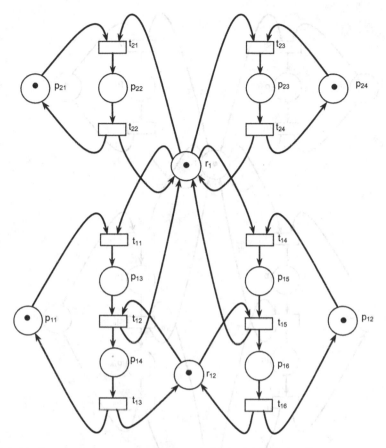

Fig. 5.4 The integrated augmented marked graph (N', M_0', R') obtained by composing $(N_1, M_{10}; R_1)$ and $(N_2, M_{20}; R_2)$ in Fig. 5.3

so does every place in (N_2', M_{20}'). Obviously, (N', M_0') is the composite net of (N_1', M_{10}') and (N_2', M_{20}'), and therefore, every place in (N', M_0') belongs to a cycle. Hence, $(N, M_0; R)$ is a proper augmented marked graph. □

Property 5.2 shows that the integrated augmented marked graph obtained by composing two proper augmented marked graphs will be a proper augmented marked graph. On the other hand, if one of the augmented marked graphs to be composed is not a proper augmented marked graph, then the integrated augmented marked graph will not be a proper augmented marked graph.

Example 5.3 Consider the two augmented marked graphs $(N_1, M_{10}; R_1)$ and $(N_2, M_{20}; R_2)$ shown in Fig. 5.1, and the integrated augmented marked graph $(N, M_0; R)$ shown in Fig. 5.2. Both $(N_1, M_{10}; R_1)$ and $(N_2, M_{20}; R_2)$ are proper augmented marked graphs. $(N, M_0; R)$ is also a proper augmented marked graph.

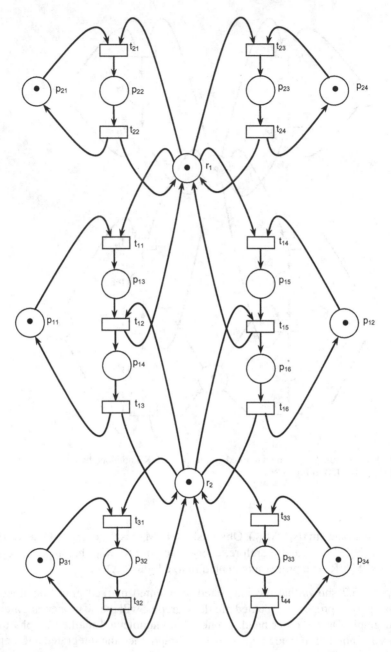

Fig. 5.5 The final integrated augmented marked graph $(N, M_0; R)$ obtained by composing $(N_3, M_{30}; R_3)$ and $(N', M_0'; R')$ in Figs. 5.3 and 5.4

Example 5.4 Consider the three augmented marked graphs $(N_1, M_{10}; R_1)$, $(N_2, M_{20}; R_2)$ and $(N_3, M_{30}; R_3)$ shown in Fig. 5.3, and the integrated augmented marked graphs $(N', M_0'; R')$ and $(N, M_0; R)$ shown in Figs. 5.4 and 5.5 respectively. $(N_1, M_{10}; R_1)$, $(N_2, M_{20}; R_2)$ and $(N_3, M_{30}; R_3)$ are proper augmented marked graphs. Both $(N', M_0'; R')$ and $(N, M_0; R)$ are also proper augmented marked graphs.

Example 5.5 Figure 5.6 shows two augmented marked graphs $(N_1, M_{10}; R_1)$ and $(N_2, M_{20}; R_2)$, where $r_{11} \in R_1$ and $r_{21} \in R_2$ refer to the same common resource to be fused. Figure 5.7 shows the integrated augmented marked graph $(N, M_0; R)$, obtained by composing $(N_1, M_{10}; R_1)$ and $(N_2, M_{20}; R_2)$ via their common resource places, where $r_1 \in R$ is the fused place of r_{11} and r_{21}. $(N_1, M_{10}; R_1)$ is a proper augmented marked graph whilst $(N_2, M_{20}; R_2)$ is not. $(N, M_0; R)$ is not a proper augmented marked graph.

5.2 Preservation of Liveness and Reversibility

This section focus on the preservation of liveness and reversibility in the composition of augmented marked graphs.

Huang found that, for the composition of two augmented marked graphs, the liveness of the integrated augmented marked graph implies the liveness of the two augmented marked graphs to be composed [1]. We also provide an alternative way to prove this property, as follows.

Property 5.3 Let $(N, M_0; R)$ be the integrated augmented marked graph obtained by composing two augmented marked graphs $(N_1, M_{10}; R_1)$ and $(N_2, M_{20}; R_2)$ via a set of common resource places $\{(r_{11}, r_{21}), (r_{12}, r_{22}), \ldots, (r_{1k}, r_{2k})\}$, where $r_{11}, r_{12}, \ldots, r_{1k} \in R_1$ and $r_{21}, r_{22}, \ldots, r_{2k} \in R_2$. $(N_1, M_{10}; R_1)$ and $(N_2, M_{20}; R_2)$ are live if $(N, M_0; R)$ is live.

Proof (by contradiction) Suppose $(N_1, M_{10}; R_1)$ and $(N_2, M_{20}; R_2)$ are live, but $(N, M_0; R)$ is not live. According to Property 3.9, there exists a siphon S in $(N, M_0; R)$ such that S would eventually become empty. There are two possible cases of S. For the first case, S does not contain any fused resource places from $(N_1, M_{10}; R_1)$ and $(N_2, M_{20}; R_2)$. Hence, S should appear in $(N_1, M_{10}; R_1)$ or $(N_2, M_{20}; R_2)$. However, since $(N_1, M_{10}; R_1)$ and $(N_2, M_{20}; R_2)$ are live, according to Property 3.9, S would never become empty. For the second case, S contains the fused resource places from $(N_1, M_{10}; R_1)$ and $(N_2, M_{20}; R_2)$. Let $r_1 \in R_1$ and $r_2 \in R_2$ be the common resource places to be fused. According to Property 3.5, there exists a siphon S_1 in $(N_1, M_{10}; R_1)$ such that S_1 contains r_1. There also exists a siphon S_2 in $(N_2, M_{20}; R_2)$ such that S_2 contains r_2. Since both $(N_1, M_{10}; R_1)$ and $(N_2, M_{20}; R_2)$ are live, according to Property 3.9, both S_1 and S_2 would never become empty. Since S contains S_1 and S_2, S would never become empty. $\square$

Example 5.6 Consider the three augmented marked graphs $(N_1, M_{10}; R_1)$, $(N_2, M_{20}; R_2)$ and $(N_3, M_{30}; R_3)$ shown in Fig. 5.3, and the integrated augmented marked

Fig. 5.6 Augmented
marked graphs $(N_1, M_{10},$
$R_1)$ and (N_2, M_{20}, R_2) with
common resource places

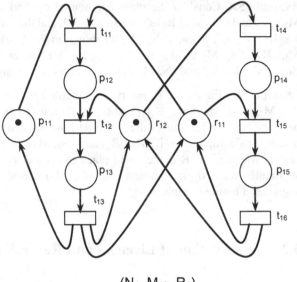

(N_1, M_{10}, R_1)

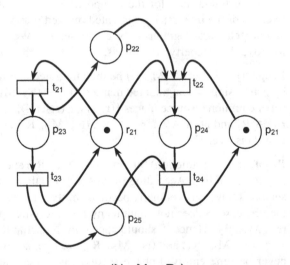

(N_2, M_{20}, R_2)

graphs $(N', M_0'; R')$ and $(N, M_0; R)$ shown in Figs. 5.4 and 5.5 respectively. $(N_1,$
$M_{10}; R_1), (N_2, M_{20}; R_2)$ and $(N_3, M_{30}; R_3)$ are live. $(N', M_0'; R')$ is live. $(N, M_0; R)$ is
also live.

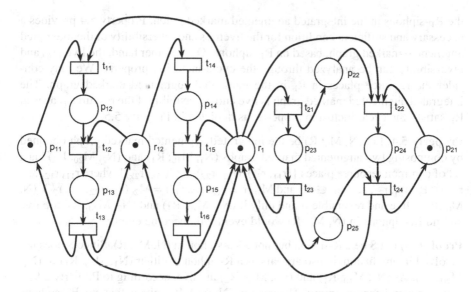

Fig. 5.7 The integrated augmented marked graph obtained by composing the augmented marked graphs in Fig. 5.6

Example 5.7 Consider the two augmented marked graphs $(N_1, M_{10}; R_1)$ and $(N_2, M_{20}; R_2)$ shown in Fig. 5.6, and the integrated augmented marked graph $(N, M_0; R)$ shown in Fig. 5.7. $(N_2, M_{20}; R_2)$ is live, whilst $(N_1, M_{10}; R_1)$ is not. $(N, M_0; R)$ is not live.

In the literature, the studies on preservation of liveness and reversibility in the composition of augmented marked graphs are based on siphons [2–4].

In the following, we define R_F as the set of fused resource places in the integrated augmented marked graph, and R_F-siphons as the minimal siphons involving places in R_F in the integrated augmented marked graph. R_F-siphons are then used for analyzing the preservation of liveness and reversibility in the composition of augmented marked graphs.

Definition 5.2 Let $(N, M_0; R)$ be the integrated augmented marked graph obtained by composing two augmented marked graphs $(N_1, M_{10}; R_1)$ and $(N_2, M_{20}; R_2)$ via a set of common resource places $\{(r_{11}, r_{21}), (r_{12}, r_{22}), \ldots, (r_{1k}, r_{2k})\}$, where $r_{11} \in R_1$ and $r_{21} \in R_2$ are fused into one resource place r_1, $r_{12} \in R_1$ and $r_{22} \in R_2$ are fused into r_2, $r_{13} \in R_1$ and $r_{23} \in R_2$ are fused into r_3, and so on. $R_F = \{r_1, r_2, \ldots r_k\} \subseteq R$ is called the set of fused resource places.

Definition 5.3 For an integrated augmented marked graph $(N, M_0; R)$ obtained by composing two augmented marked graphs via a set of common resource places, a minimal siphon is called a R_F-siphon if and only if it contains at least one place in R_F, where R_F is the set of fused resource places in $(N, M_0; R)$.

In analyzing the liveness and reversibility of the integrated augmented marked graph, if the augmented marked graphs to be composed are live, we may consider the R_F-siphons in the integrated augmented marked graph. Property 5.4 provides a necessary and sufficient condition for the liveness and reversibility of the integrated augmented marked graph, based on R_F-siphons. On the other hand, the liveness and reversibility can be analyzed through the cycle-inclusion property. We may consider the resource places in R_F in the integrated augmented marked graph. The integrated augmented marked graph is live and reversibility if the resource places in R_F satisfy the cycle-inclusion property, as depicted in Property 5.5.

Property 5.4 Let $(N, M_0; R)$ be the integrated augmented marked graph obtained by composing two augmented marked graphs $(N_1, M_{10}; R_1)$ and $(N_2, M_{20}; R_2)$ via a set of common resource places $\{(r_{11}, r_{21}), (r_{12}, r_{22}), \ldots, (r_{1k}, r_{2k})\}$ where $r_{11}, r_{12}, \ldots, r_{1k} \in R_1, r_{21}, r_{22}, \ldots, r_{2k} \in R_2$ and $M_{10}(r_{11}, r_{12}, \ldots, r_{1k}) = M_{20}(r_{21}, r_{22}, \ldots, r_{2k})$. $(N, M_0; R)$ is live and reversible if and only if $(N_1, M_{10}; R_1)$ and $(N_2, M_{20}; R_2)$ are live and no R_F-siphons in $(N, M_0; R)$ would eventually become empty.

Proof ($\Leftarrow$) Let S be a R-siphon but not a R_F-siphon in $(N, M_0; R)$. Since S does not involved in any fusion, it also appears as a R-siphon in either $(N_1, M_{10}; R_1)$ or $(N_2, M_{20}; R_2)$. As $(N_1, M_{10}; R_1)$ and $(N_2, M_{20}; R_2)$ are live, according to Property 3.9, S would never become empty. Hence, for $(N, M_0; R)$, given that no R_F-siphons eventually become empty, no R-siphons would eventually become empty. According to Property 3.9, $(N, M_0; R)$ is live and reversible. ($\Rightarrow$) It follows from Property 5.3 that $(N_1, M_{10}; R_1)$ and $(N_2, M_{20}; R_2)$ are live. Moreover, according to Property 3.9, no R_F-siphons eventually become empty. $\square$

Based on Properties 3.6 and 5.4, we derive a strategy for checking the liveness and reversibility of the integrated augmented marked graph obtained by the composition of two augmented marked graphs, as shown in Algorithm 5.1.

Algorithm 5.1 Checking the liveness and reversibility of the integrated augmented marked graph $(N, M_0; R)$, obtained by composing two augmented marked graphs $(N_1, M_{10}; R_1)$ and $(N_2, M_{20}; R_2)$.

Step 1.   Find all the R-siphons in $(N_1, M_{10}; R_1)$ based on $\Omega_{N1}[R_1]$. Likewise, find all the R-siphons in $(N_2, M_{20}; R_2)$ based on $\Omega_{N2}[R_2]$.

Step 2.   If all the R-siphons in $(N_1, M_{10}; R_1)$ and $(N_1, M_{10}; R_1)$ would never become empty, then proceed to Step 3. Otherwise, report that $(N, M_0; R)$ is neither live nor reversible.

Step 3.   Find all the R_F-siphons in $(N, M_0; R)$ based on $\Omega_N[R_F]$.

Step 4.   If all the R_F-siphons in $(N, M_0; R)$ would never become empty, then report $(N, M_0; R)$ is live nor reversible. Otherwise, report that $(N, M_0; R)$ is neither live nor reversible.

Property 5.5 Let $(N_1, M_{10}; R_1)$ and $(N_2, M_{20}; R_2)$ be augmented marked graphs, where every place in R_1 and R_2 satisfies the cycle-inclusion property. Let $(N, M_0; R)$ be the integrated augmented marked graph obtained by composing $(N_1, M_{10}; R_1)$

and $(N_2, M_{20}; R_2)$ via their common resource places. $(N, M_0; R)$ is live and reversible if every place in R_F satisfies the cycle-inclusion property.

Proof For $(N, M_0; R)$, there are two possible cases for each place $r \in R$. In case $r \in R_F$, r satisfies the cycle-inclusion property as given. In case $r \notin R_F$, r also exists in R_1 (or R_2), and satisfies the cycle-inclusion property, where for any set of cycles $Y \subseteq \Omega_{N1}[r]$ (or $\Omega_{N2}[r]$) such that Y is conflict-free, $\dot{r} \subseteq T[Y] \Rightarrow r^\bullet \subseteq T[Y]$. We have $\Omega_N[r] = \Omega_{N1}[r]$ (or $\Omega_{N2}[r]$). Then, for any set of cycles $Y' \subseteq \Omega_{N1}[r]$ such that Y' is conflict-free, $\dot{r} \subseteq T[Y'] \Rightarrow r^\bullet \subseteq T[Y']$. r also satisfies the cycle-inclusion property. Then, every place in R satisfies the cycle-inclusion property. It follows from Property 3.17 that $(N, M_0; R)$ is live and reversible. $\square$

Based on Properties 3.6, 5.4 and 5.5, we revise the strategy for checking the liveness and reversibility of the integrated augmented marked graph obtained by the composition of two augmented marked graphs. Algorithm 5.2 shows the revised algorithm where the checking is based on cycle-inclusion property.

Algorithm 5.2 Checking the liveness and reversibility of the integrated augmented marked graph $(N, M_0; R)$, obtained by composing two augmented marked graphs $(N_1, M_{10}; R_1)$ and $(N_2, M_{20}; R_2)$.

Step 1. For $(N_1, M_{10}; R_1)$, check if the places in R_1 satisfy the cycle-inclusion property. Likewise, for $(N_2, M_{20}; R_2)$, check if the places in R_2 satisfy the cycle-inclusion property.

Step 2. Suppose the places in R_1 and R_2 satisfy the cycle-inclusion property. Then, for $(N, M_0; R)$, check if the places in R_F satisfy the cycle-inclusion property.

Step 3. If the places in R_F satisfy the cycle-inclusion property, report that $(N, M_0; R)$ is live and reversible. Otherwise, proceed to Step 4.

Step 4. Find all the R-siphons in $(N_1, M_{10}; R_1)$ based on $\Omega_{N1}[R_1]$. Likewise, find all the R-siphons in $(N_2, M_{20}; R_2)$ based on $\Omega_{N2}[R_2]$.

Step 5. If all the R-siphons in $(N_1, M_{10}; R_1)$ and $(N_1, M_{10}; R_1)$ would never become empty, then proceed to Step 6. Otherwise, report that $(N, M_0; R)$ is neither live nor reversible.

Step 6. Find all the R_F-siphons in $(N, M_0; R)$ based on $\Omega_N[R_F]$.

Step 7. If all the R_F-siphons in $(N, M_0; R)$ would never become empty, then report $(N, M_0; R)$ is live nor reversible. Otherwise, report that $(N, M_0; R)$ is neither live nor reversible.

Property 5.6 Let $(N_1, M_{10}; R_1)$ and $(N_2, M_{20}; R_2)$ be augmented marked graphs, satisfying the siphon-trap property. Let $(N, M_0; R)$ be the integrated augmented marked graph obtained by composing $(N_1, M_{10}; R_1)$ and $(N_2, M_{20}; R_2)$ via their common resource places. $(N, M_0; R)$ is live and reversible if every place in R_F contains a marked trap.

Proof It simply follows Properties 3.16 and 5.5. □

Example 5.8 Consider the two augmented marked graphs $(N_1, M_{10}; R_1)$ and $(N_2, M_{20}; R_2)$ shown in Fig. 5.1, and the integrated augmented marked graph $(N, M_0; R)$ shown in Fig. 5.2. $(N_2, M_{20}; R_2)$ is live whilst $(N_1, M_{10}; R_1)$ is not. For $(N, M_0; R)$, where $R_F = \{r_1\}$, $S = \{r_1, r_{12}, p_{13}, p_{15}, p_{22}, p_{23}\}$ is a R_F-siphon. S would become empty on firing t_{11} and t_{14}. $(N, M_0; R)$ is not live.

Example 5.9 Consider the three augmented marked graphs $(N_1, M_{10}; R_1)$, $(N_2, M_{20}; R_2)$ and $(N_3, M_{30}; R_3)$ shown in Fig. 5.3, and the integrated augmented marked graphs $(N', M_0'; R')$ and $(N, M_0; R)$ shown in Figs. 5.4 and 5.5 respectively. $(N_1, M_{10}; R_1)$, $(N_2, M_{20}; R_2)$ and $(N_3, M_{30}; R_3)$ are live. For $(N', M_0'; R')$, where $R_F' = \{r_1\}$, $S_1 = \{r_1, p_{13}, p_{15}, p_{22}, p_{23}\}$ is a R_F-siphon which would never become empty. $(N', M_0'; R')$ is live. For $(N, M_0; R)$, where $R_F = \{r_2\}$, $S_2 = \{r_2, p_{14}, p_{16}, p_{32}, p_{33}\}$ is a R_F-siphon which would never become empty. Then, $(N, M_0; R)$ is live.

Let us analyze the liveness and reversibility of $(N, M_0; R)$, based on the cycle-inclusion property. For $(N_1, M_{10}; R_1)$, the places in R_1 satisfy the cycle-inclusion property. Likewise, for $(N_2, M_{20}; R_2)$ and $(N_3, M_{30}; R_3)$, the places in R_2 and R_3 satisfy the cycle-inclusion property. $(N_1, M_{10}; R_1)$, $(N_2, M_{20}; R_2)$ and $(N_3, M_{30}; R_3)$ all satisfy the siphon-trap property, and hence, are live and reversible. Consider $(N', M_0'; R')$, where $R_F' = \{r_1\}$. r_1 satisfies the cycle-inclusion. $(N', M_0'; R')$ satisfies the siphon-trap property, and hence, is live and reversible. Next, consider the final integrated augmented marked graph $(N, M_0; R)$, where $R_F = \{r_2\}$. r_2 satisfies the cycle-inclusion. $(N, M_0; R)$ satisfies the siphon-trap property, and hence, is live and reversible.

5.3 Preservation of Boundedness and Conservativeness

This section focus on the preservation of boundedness and conservativeness in the composition of augmented marked graphs.

In the literature, Huang found that boundedness is preserved in the composition of augmented marked graphs [1]. Cheung further found that conservativeness is preserved in the composition of augmented marked graphs [2–4].

Property 5.7 Let $(N, M_0; R)$ be the integrated augmented marked graph obtained by composing two augmented marked graphs $(N_1, M_{10}; R_1)$ and $(N_2, M_{20}; R_2)$ via a set of common resource places $\{(r_{11}, r_{21}), (r_{12}, r_{22}), \ldots, (r_{1k}, r_{2k})\}$ where $r_{11}, r_{12}, \ldots, r_{1k} \in R_1, r_{21}, r_{22}, \ldots, r_{2k} \in R_2$ and $M_{10}(r_{11}, r_{12}, \ldots, r_{1k}) = M_{20}(r_{21}, r_{22}, \ldots, r_{2k})$. $(N, M_0; R)$ is bounded if and only if $(N_1, M_{10}; R_1)$ and $(N_2, M_{20}; R_2)$ are bounded [1].

Lemma 5.1 Let $N = \langle P, T, F \rangle$ be a PT-net and $N' = \langle P', T', F' \rangle$ be the PT-net obtained from N after fusing a set of places $Q = \{q_1, q_2, \ldots, q_n\} \subset P$ into a single place $r \in P'$. If there exists a place invariant α of N such that $\alpha[q_1] = \alpha[q_2] = \ldots = \alpha[q_n] = j \geq 0$, then there also exists a place invariant α' of N' such that $\alpha'[r] = j$ and $\alpha'[s] = \alpha[s]$ for any $s \in P' \backslash \{r\} = P \backslash Q$.

Proof Let V be the incidence matrix of N. Then, the incidence matrix V' of N' satisfies that $V'[r] = \Sigma_{i=1,2,\ldots,n}V[q_i]$ and $V'[s] = V[s]$ for any $s \in P'\backslash\{r\} = P\backslash Q$. Since α is a place invariant of N, $\alpha V = 0$. Let α' be a place vector of N' such that $\alpha'[r] = \alpha[q_1] = \alpha[q_2] = \ldots = \alpha[q_n] = j$ and $\alpha'[s] = \alpha[s]$ for every $s \in P'\backslash\{r\} = P\backslash Q$. Then, $\alpha'V' = \alpha'[r]V'[r] + \Sigma_{p \in (P'\backslash\{r\})}\alpha'[p]V'[p] = \Sigma_{i=1,2,\ldots,n}\alpha[q_i]V[q_i] + \Sigma_{p \in (P\backslash Q)}\alpha[p]V[p] = \alpha V = 0$. Hence, α' is a place invariant of N'. $\square$

Lemma 5.2 Let $N = \langle P, T, F \rangle$ be a PT-net and $N' = \langle P', T', F' \rangle$ be the PT-net obtained from N after fusing a set of places $Q = \{ q_1, q_2, \ldots, q_n \} \subset P$ into a single place $r \in P'$. If there exists a place invariant α' of N' such that $\alpha'[r] = j \geq 0$, then there also exists a place invariant α of N such that $\alpha[q_1] = \alpha[q_2] = \ldots = \alpha[q_n] = j$ and $\alpha[s] = \alpha'[s]$ for any $s \in P\backslash Q = P'\backslash\{r\}$.

Proof Let V be the incidence matrix of N. Then, the incidence matrix V' of N' satisfies that $V'[r] = \Sigma_{i=1,2,\ldots,n}V[q_i]$ and $V'[s] = V[s]$ for any $s \in P'\backslash\{r\} = P\backslash Q$. Since α' is a place invariant of N', $\alpha'V' = 0$. Let α be a place vector of N such that $\alpha[q_1] = \alpha[q_2] = \ldots = \alpha[q_n] = j$ and $\alpha[s] = \alpha'[s]$ for every $s \in P\backslash Q = P'\backslash\{r\}$. Then, $\alpha V = \Sigma_{i=1,2,\ldots,n}\alpha[q_i]V[q_i] + \Sigma_{p \in (P\backslash Q)}\alpha[p]V[p] = \alpha'[r]V'[r] + \Sigma_{p \in (P'\backslash\{r\})}\alpha'[p]V'[p] = \alpha'V'$. Hence, α is a place invariant of N. $\square$

Property 5.8 Let $(N, M_0; R)$ be the integrated augmented marked graph obtained by composing two augmented marked graphs $(N_1, M_{10}; R_1)$ and $(N_2, M_{20}; R_2)$ via a set of common resource places $\{(r_{11}, r_{21}), (r_{12}, r_{22}), \ldots, (r_{1k}, r_{2k})\}$, where $r_{11}, r_{12}, \ldots, r_{1k} \in R_1, r_{21}, r_{22}, \ldots, r_{2k} \in R_2$ and $M_{10}(r_{11}, r_{12}, \ldots, r_{1k}) = M_{20}(r_{21}, r_{22}, \ldots, r_{2k})$. $(N, M_0; R)$ is conservative if and only if $(N_1, M_{10}; R_1)$ and $(N_2, M_{20}; R_2)$ are conservative.

Proof Suppose $N_1 = \langle P_1, T_1, F_1 \rangle$ and $N_2 = \langle P_2, T_2, F_2 \rangle$. Let $N' = \langle P', T', F' \rangle$ be a PT-net where $P' = P_1 \cup P_2$, $T' = P_1 \cup P_2$ and $T' = T_1 \cup T_2$. N is obtained from N' by fusing $\{ r_{11}, r_{21} \}$ into r_1, (r_{12}, r_{22}), into r_2, $\ldots$, (r_{1k}, r_{2k}), into r_k. Let V and V' be the incidence matrices of N and N' respectively. ($\Leftarrow$) Since N_1 and N_2 are conservative, there exists place invariants $\alpha_1 > 0$ of N_1 and $\alpha_2 > 0$ of N_2. $\alpha' = (\alpha_1 + \alpha_2) > 0$ is a place invariant of N'. According to Lemma 5.1, there exists a place invariant $\alpha > 0$ of N, and N is conservative. ($\Rightarrow$) Since N is conservative, there exists a place invariant $\alpha > 0$ of N. According to Lemma 5.2, there exists a place invariant $\alpha' > 0$ of N'. Let $\alpha' = \alpha_1 + \alpha_2$, where α_1 and α_2 are place invariants of N_1 and N_2. Since $\alpha' > 0$, $\alpha_1 > 0$ and $\alpha_2 > 0$. Hence, N_1 and N_2 are conservative. $\square$

Property 5.9 Let $(N, M_0; R)$ be the integrated augmented marked graph obtained by composing two augmented marked graphs $(N_1, M_{10}; R_1)$ and $(N_2, M_{20}; R_2)$ via a set of common resource places $\{(r_{11}, r_{21}), (r_{12}, r_{22}), \ldots, (r_{1k}, r_{2k})\}$, where $r_{11}, r_{12}, \ldots, r_{1k} \in R_1, r_{21}, r_{22}, \ldots, r_{2k} \in R_2$ and $M_{10}(r_{11}, r_{12}, \ldots, r_{1k}) = M_{20}(r_{21}, r_{22}, \ldots, r_{2k})$. $(N, M_0; R)$ is bounded and conservative if and only if $(N_1, M_{10}; R_1)$ and $(N_2, M_{20}; R_2)$ are bounded and conservative.

Proof It simply follows Properties 5.7 and 5.8. □

Example 5.10 Consider the augmented marked graphs $(N_1, M_{10}; R_1)$ and $(N_2, M_{20}; R_2)$ shown in Fig. 5.1, and the integrated augmented marked graph $(N, M_0; R)$ shown in Fig. 5.2. Both $(N_1, M_{10}; R_1)$ and $(N_2, M_{20}; R_2)$ are bounded and conservative. There exists a place invariant $\alpha_1 > 0$ in $(N_1, M_{10}; R_1)$, and a place invariant $\alpha_2 > 0$ in $(N_2, M_{20}; R_2)$. There also exists a place invariant $\alpha > 0$ in $(N, M_0; R)$, and hence, $(N, M_0; R)$ is bounded and conservative.

Example 5.11 Consider the augmented marked graphs $(N_1, M_{10}; R_1)$, $(N_2, M_{20}; R_2)$ and $(N_3, M_{30}; R_3)$ shown in Fig. 5.3, and the integrated augmented marked graph $(N, M_0; R)$ shown in Fig. 5.5. $(N_1, M_{10}; R_1)$, $(N_2, M_{20}; R_2)$ and $(N_3, M_{30}; R_3)$ are bounded and conservative. There exist place invariants $\alpha_1 > 0$ in $(N_1, M_{10}; R_1)$, $\alpha_2 > 0$ in $(N_2, M_{20}; R_2)$ and $\alpha_3 > 0$ in $(N_3, M_{30}; R_3)$. There also exists a place invariant $\alpha > 0$ in $(N, M_0; R)$. $(N, M_0; R)$ is bounded and conservative.

Example 5.12 Consider the augmented marked graphs $(N_1, M_{10}; R_1)$ and $(N_2, M_{20}; R_2)$ shown in Fig. 5.6, and the integrated augmented marked graph $(N, M_0; R)$ shown in Fig. 5.7. $(N_1, M_{10}; R_1)$ is bounded and conservative. There exists a place invariant $\alpha_1 > 0$ in $(N_1, M_{10}; R_1)$. However, $(N_2, M_{20}; R_2)$ is neither bounded and conservative. For $(N_2, M_{20}; R_2)$, p_{22} and p_{25} are not bounded on firing $\langle\, t_{21}, t_{23}, t_{21}, t_{23}, t_{21}, t_{23}, \ldots \,\rangle$. $(N, M_0; R)$ is neither bounded nor conservative, where p_{22} and p_{25} are not bounded on firing $\langle\, t_{21}, t_{23}, t_{21}, t_{23}, t_{21}, t_{23}, \ldots \,\rangle$.

Property 5.10 Let $(N, M_0; R)$ be the integrated augmented marked graph obtained by composing two proper augmented marked graphs $(N_1, M_{10}; R_1)$ and $(N_2, M_{20}; R_2)$ via a set of common resource places $\{(r_{11}, r_{21}), (r_{12}, r_{22}), \ldots, (r_{1k}, r_{2k})\}$, where $r_{11}, r_{12}, \ldots, r_{1k} \in R_1, r_{21}, r_{22}, \ldots, r_{2k} \in R_2$ and $M_{10}(r_{11}, r_{12}, \ldots, r_{1k}) = M_{20}(r_{21}, r_{22}, \ldots, r_{2k})$. $(N, M_0; R)$ is bounded and conservative.

Proof Since $(N_1, M_{10}; R_1)$ and $(N_2, M_{20}; R_2)$ are proper augmented marked graphs, according to Property 4.3, $(N_1, M_{10}; R_1)$ and $(N_2, M_{20}; R_2)$ are bounded and conservative. It follows from Property 5.7 that $(N, M_0; R)$ is bounded and conservative. □

References

1. K.S. Cheung, K.O. Chow, Compositional synthesis of augmented marked graphs, in *Proceedings of the IEEE International Conference on Control and Automation* (IEEE Press, 2007), pp. 2810–2814
2. K.S. Cheung, Composition of augmented marked graphs and its application to component-based system design. Inf. Technol. Control **36**(3), 310–317 (2007)
3. K.S. Cheung, Compositional synthesis of distributed system components based on augmented marked graphs. J. Comput. Sci. Technol. **8**(1), 34–40 (2008)
4. H.J. Huang, L. Jiao, T.Y. Cheung, Property-preserving composition of augmented marked graphs that share common resources, in *Proceedings of the International Conference on Robotics and Automation* (IEEE Press, 2003)

Chapter 6
The Dining Philosophers Problem

This chapter illustrates the theories in Chaps. 3–5, using the well-known dining philosophers problem. It starts with modelling the dining philosophers problem with augmented marked graphs. The system properties, including liveness, boundedness, reversibility and conservativeness, are then analyzed. We also show the composition of augmented marked graphs for modelling and analyzing the dining philosophers problem. The beauty of property-preserving composition is discussed.

6.1 The Dining Philosophers Problem

Introduced by Dijkstra, the dining philosophers problem is often used in studying issues of concurrency in systems [1]. In the literature, it is also used for modelling and analyzing shared-resource systems with augmented marked graphs [2–5]. Two versions of the dining philosophers problem are used for investigation in the subsequent sections of this chapter.

The Dining Philosophers Problem (Version 1) There are four meditating philosophers, namely, H_1, H_2, H_3 and H_4, sitting around a circular table for dinner. The foods are placed at the centre of the table, for the philosophers to share. Each philosopher needs to use a pair of chopsticks to get the food to his own plate. There are four pieces of chopsticks, namely, C_1, C_2, C_3 and C_4, shared by the philosophers. Figure 6.1 shows the table setting. For a philosopher to get the food, both the chopstick at the left-hand side and the chopstick at the right-hand side must be available. The philosopher grasps both chopsticks simultaneously, and then takes the food to his own plate to eat. The chopsticks are then released and returned to their original positions simultaneously.

The Dining Philosophers Problem (Version 2) This version 2 is a modified version. The table setting is the same as Version 1, as shown in Fig. 6.1, whereas the sequence of getting the chopsticks and food is different. The four meditating philosophers share the chopsticks to get the food to their own plates. For a

K.S. Cheung, *Augmented Marked Graphs*, DOI 10.1007/978-3-319-06428-4_6,
© Springer International Publishing Switzerland 2014

Fig. 6.1 The dining
philosophers problem

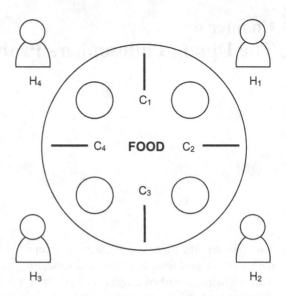

philosopher to get the food, the chopstick at the right-hand side must be available. The philosopher grasps the chopstick. Then, if the chopstick at the left-hand side is also available, the philosopher grasps it to get both chopsticks. Otherwise, the philosopher waits until the chopstick at the left-hand side become available, while holding the chopstick at the right-hand side. Once both chopsticks are grasped, the philosopher uses the chopsticks to take the food to his own plate to eat. The chopsticks are then released and returned to their original positions simultaneously.

Consider the dining philosophers problem from the systems perspective. The chopsticks are the common resources shared among the philosophers, for example, C_1 is shared between H_1 and H_4, C_2 is shared between H_1 and H_2, and so on for the other chopsticks. In contrary, the plate in the front of each philosopher is not a common resource, since it is exclusively used by the philosopher. While one philosopher is grasping the chopsticks to take the food to his own plate, other philosophers can do the same simultaneously. These are concurrent processes. Hence, the dining philosophers problem can be considered as a system, involving shared resources and concurrent processes.

6.2 Modelling and Analysis Using Augmented Marked Graphs

This section illustrates how the dining philosophers problem can be modelled and analyzed using augmented marked graphs. Example 6.1 illustrates the dining philosophers problem (version 1) while Example 6.2 illustrates the dining philosophers problem (version 2).

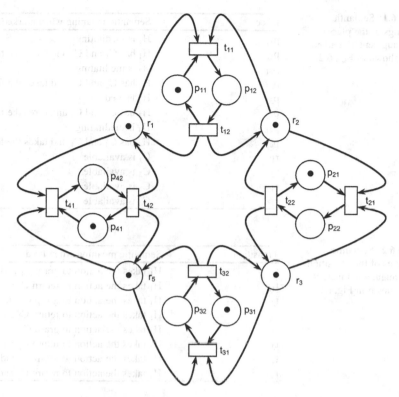

Fig. 6.2 An augmented marked graph $(N, M_0; R)$ representing the dining philosophers problem (version 1)

Example 6.1 Consider the dining philosophers problem (version 1). It is modelled as an augmented marked graph $(N, M_0; R)$, where $R = \{r_1, r_2, r_3, r_4, r_5, r_6\}$ represents the common resources, C_1, C_2, C_3 and C_4. Figure 6.2 shows $(N, M_0; R)$ while Tables 6.1 and 6.2 state the semantic meanings of places and transitions, respectively.

Let us investigate the liveness and reversibility of $(N, M_0; R)$ through siphons. For $(N, M_0; R)$, there are 4 R-siphons, namely, $\{r_1, p_{42}, p_{12}\}$, $\{r_2, p_{12}, p_{22}\}$, $\{r_3, p_{22}, p_{32}\}$ and $\{r_4, p_{32}, p_{42}\}$, and 4 NR-siphons, namely, $\{p_{11}, p_{12}\}$, $\{p_{21}, p_{22}\}$, $\{p_{31}, p_{32}\}$ and $\{p_{41}, p_{42}\}$. Each of these R-siphons contains a marked trap, and would never become empty. $(N, M_0; R)$ satisfies the siphon-trap property. According to Properties 3.11, 3.12, 3.13 and 3.14, $(N, M_0; R)$ is live and reversible.

The liveness and reversibility of $(N, M_0; R)$ can be studied through the cycle-inclusion property. Consider r_1. For any set of cycles $Y \subseteq \Omega_N[r_1]$ such that Y is conflict-free, ${}^\bullet p \subseteq T[Y] \Rightarrow p^\bullet \subseteq T[Y]$. Hence, r_1 satisfies the cycle-inclusion property. Likewise, r_2, r_3, r_4, r_5 and r_6 satisfy the cycle-inclusion property. Since every place $r \in R$ satisfies the cycle-inclusion property, according to Property 3.17, $(N, M_0; R)$ is live and reversible.

Table 6.1 Semantic meanings of the places in the augmented marked graph shown in Fig. 6.2

Place	Semantic meaning when marked
p_{11}	H_1 is meditating
p_{12}	H_1 has C_1 and C_2 and takes the food
p_{21}	H_2 is meditating
p_{22}	H_2 has C_2 and C_3 and takes the food
p_{31}	H_3 is meditating
p_{32}	H_3 has C_3 and C_4 and takes the food
p_{41}	H_4 is meditating
p_{42}	H_4 has C_4 and C_1 and takes the food
r_1	C_1 is available
r_2	C_2 is available
r_3	C_3 is available
r_4	C_4 is available

Table 6.2 Semantic meanings of the transitions in the augmented marked graph shown in Fig. 6.2

Transition	Semantic meaning when fired
t_{11}	H_1 takes the action to grasp C_1 and C_2
t_{12}	H_1 takes the action to return C_1 and C_2
t_{21}	H_1 takes the action to grasp C_2 and C_3
t_{22}	H_1 takes the action to return C_2 and C_3
t_{31}	H_1 takes the action to grasp C_3 and C_4
t_{32}	H_1 takes the action to return C_3 and C_4
t_{41}	H_1 takes the action to grasp C_4 and C_1
t_{42}	H_1 takes the action to return C_4 and C_1

Let us investigate the boundedness and conservativeness of $(N, M_0; R)$. Let (N', M_0') be the R-transform of $(N, M_0; R)$. For (N', M_0'), every place belongs to a cycle. Then, according to Property 3.22, $(N, M_0; R)$ is bounded and conservative. $(N, M_0; R)$ is also a proper augmented marked graph. It follows from Property 4.9 that $(N, M_0; R)$ is both T-coverable and P-coverable.

Example 6.2 Consider the dining philosophers problem (version 2). It is modelled as an augmented marked graph $(N, M_0; R)$, where $R = \{r_1, r_2, r_3, r_4\}$ represents the common resources, C_1, C_2, C_3 and C_4. Figure 6.3 shows $(N, M_0; R)$ while Tables 6.3 and 6.4 state the semantic meanings of places and transitions, respectively.

Let us investigate the liveness and reversibility of $(N, M_0; R)$ through siphons. There exists a R-siphon, $S = \{r_1, p_{13}, r_2, p_{23}, r_3, p_{33}, r_4, p_{43}\}$, which would become empty after firing $\langle t_{11}, t_{12}, t_{13}, t_{14} \rangle$. According to Property 3.11, $(N, M_0; R)$ is neither live nor reversible. Deadlock would occur after firing $\langle t_{11}, t_{12}, t_{13}, t_{14} \rangle$. Since S does not contain any trap, $(N, M_0; R)$ does not satisfy the siphon-trap property. Consider the cycle-inclusion property of $R = \{r_1, r_2, r_3, r_4\}$. Since r_1, r_2, r_3 and r_4 do not satisfy the cycle-inclusion property, according to Property 3.16, $(N, M_0; R)$ does not satisfy the siphon-trap property.

Let us investigate the boundedness and conservativeness of $(N, M_0; R)$. Let (N', M_0') be the R-transform of $(N, M_0; R)$. For (N', M_0'), every place belongs to a cycle.

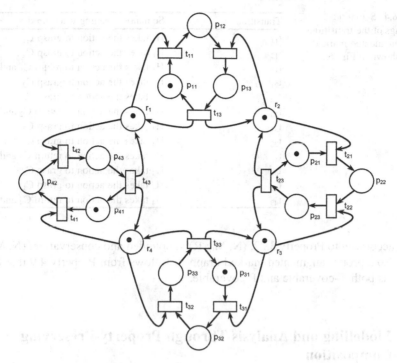

Fig. 6.3 An augmented marked graph $(N, M_0; R)$ representing the dining philosophers problem (version 2)

Place	Semantic meaning when marked
p_{11}	H_1 is meditating
p_{12}	H_1 has C_1 and prepares to pick C_2
p_{13}	H_1 has C_1 and C_2 and takes the food
p_{21}	H_2 is meditating
p_{22}	H_2 has C_2 and prepares to pick C_3
p_{23}	H_2 has C_2 and C_3 and takes the food
p_{31}	H_3 is meditating
p_{32}	H_3 has C_3 and prepares to pick C_4
p_{33}	H_3 has C_3 and C_4 and takes the food
p_{41}	H_4 is meditating
p_{42}	H_4 has C_4 and prepares to pick C_1
p_{43}	H_4 has C_4 and C_1 and takes the food
r_1	C_1 is available
r_2	C_2 is available
r_3	C_3 is available
r_4	C_4 is available

Table 6.3 Semantic meanings of the places in the augmented marked graph shown in Fig. 6.3

Table 6.4 Semantic meanings of the transitions in the augmented marked graph shown in Fig. 6.3

Transition	Semantic meaning when fired
t_{11}	H_1 takes the action to grasp C_1
t_{12}	H_1 takes the action to grasp C_2
t_{13}	H_1 takes the action to return C_1 and C_2
t_{21}	H_2 takes the action to grasp C_2
t_{22}	H_2 takes the action to grasp C_3
t_{23}	H_2 takes the action to return C_2 and C_3
t_{31}	H_3 takes the action to grasp C_3
t_{32}	H_3 takes the action to grasp C_4
t_{33}	H_3 takes the action to return C_3 and C_4
t_{41}	H_4 takes the action to grasp C_4
t_{42}	H_4 takes the action to grasp C_1
t_{43}	H_4 takes the action to return C_4 and C_1

Then, according to Property 3.22, $(N, M_0; R)$ is bounded and conservative. $(N, M_0; R)$ is also a proper augmented marked graph. It follows from Property 4.9 that $(N, M_0; R)$ is both T-coverable and P-coverable.

6.3 Modelling and Analysis Through Property-Preserving Composition

This section illustrates how the dining philosophers problem can be modelled as the composition of augmented marked graphs. Based on the preservation of properties of the composition, the system properties are analyzed. In the following, Example 6.3 shows the modelling and analysis of the dining philosophers problem (version 1) while Example 6.4 shows the modelling and analysis of version 2.

Example 6.3 Consider the dining philosophers problem (version 1). Let us regard each philosopher as a component. For philosopher H_1, the process for H_1 to grasp the chopsticks to get the food is modelled as an augmented marked graph $(N_1, M_{10}; R_1)$, where $R_1 = \{r_1, r_4\}$. Likewise, for other philosophers, we have augmented marked graphs $(N_2, M_{20}; R_2)$, $(N_3, M_{30}; R_3)$ and $(N_4, M_{40}; R_4)$, where $R_2 = \{r_1, r_2\}$, $R_3 = \{r_2, r_3\}$ and $R_4 = \{r_3, r_4\}$. Figure 6.4 shows the augmented marked graphs, while Tables 6.5 and 6.6 state the semantic meanings of places and transitions, respectively.

For $(N_1, M_{10}; R_1)$, $(N_2, M_{20}; R_2)$, $(N_3, M_{30}; R_3)$ and $(N_4, M_{40}; R_4)$, $r_{11} \in R_1$ and $r_{41} \in R_4$ refer to the same resource C_1. Likewise, $r_{12} \in R_1$ and $r_{22} \in R_2$ refer to C_2, $r_{23} \in R_2$ and $r_{33} \in R_3$ refer to C_3, and $r_{34} \in R_3$ and $r_{44} \in R_4$ refer to C_4. Figure 6.5 shows the integrated augmented marked graph $(N', M_0'; R')$ obtained by composing $(N_1, M_{10}; R_1)$ and $(N_2, M_{20}; R_2)$ via $\{(r_{12}, r_{22})\}$. Figure 6.6 shows the integrated augmented marked graph $(N'', M_0''; R'')$ obtained by composing $(N_3, M_{30}; R_3)$ and $(N_4, M_{40}; R_4)$ via $\{(r_{34}, r_{44})\}$. $(N', M_0'; R')$ and $(N'', M_0''; R'')$ are then composed via $\{(r_{11}, r_{41}), (r_{23}, r_{33})\}$. The final integrated augmented marked

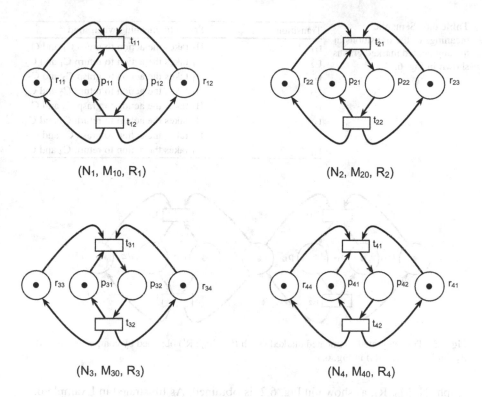

Fig. 6.4 Augmented marked graphs $(N_1, M_{10}; R_1)$, $(N_2, M_{20}; R_2)$, $(N_3, M_{30}; R_3)$ and $(N_4, M_{40}; R_4)$ representing components of the dining philosophers problem (version 1)

Table 6.5 Semantic meanings of the places in the augmented marked graphs shown in Fig. 6.4	Place	Semantic meaning when marked
	p_{11}	H_1 is meditating
	p_{12}	H_1 has C_1 and C_2 and takes the food
	p_{21}	H_2 is meditating
	p_{22}	H_2 has C_2 and C_3 and takes the food
	p_{31}	H_3 is meditating
	p_{32}	H_3 has C_3 and C_4 and takes the food
	p_{41}	H_4 is meditating
	p_{42}	H_4 has C_4 and C_1 and takes the food
	r_{11}	C_1 is available
	r_{12}	C_2 is available
	r_{22}	C_2 is available
	r_{23}	C_3 is available
	r_{33}	C_3 is available
	r_{34}	C_4 is available
	r_{41}	C_1 is available
	r_{44}	C_4 is available

Table 6.6 Semantic
meanings of the transitions in
the augmented marked graphs
shown in Fig. 6.4

Transition	Semantic meaning when fired
t_{11}	H_1 takes the action to grasp C_1 and C_2
t_{12}	H_1 takes the action to return C_1 and C_2
t_{21}	H_1 takes the action to grasp C_2 and C_3
t_{22}	H_1 takes the action to return C_2 and C_3
t_{31}	H_1 takes the action to grasp C_3 and C_4
t_{32}	H_1 takes the action to return C_3 and C_4
t_{41}	H_1 takes the action to grasp C_4 and C_1
t_{42}	H_1 takes the action to return C_4 and C_1

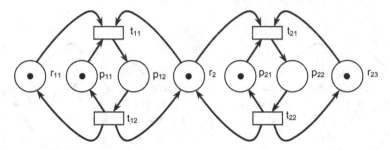

Fig. 6.5 The integrated augmented marked graph $(N', M_0'; R')$ obtained by composing $(N_1, M_{10};$ $R_1)$ and $(N_2, M_{20}; R_2)$ in Fig. 6.4

graph $(N, M_0; R)$, as shown in Fig. 6.2, is obtained. As illustrated in Example 6.1, $(N, M_0; R)$ is live, reversible, bounded and conservative.

Let us investigate the system properties, based on the preservation of properties in the composition of augmented marked graphs. Each $(N_i, M_{i0}; r_i)$ is a proper augmented marked graph. According to Properties 4.1 and 4.3, each $(N_i, M_{i0}; r_i)$ is live, bounded and conservative.

Consider the integrated augmented marked graphs $(N', M_0'; R')$ and $(N'', M_0'';$ $R'')$ shown in Figs. 6.5 and 6.6 respectively. For $(N', M_0'; R')$ where $R_F = \{r_2\}$, r_2 satisfies the cycle-inclusion property, and hence every R-siphon would never become empty. According to Properties 5.4 and 5.5, $(N', M_0'; R')$ is live and reversible. It follows from Properties 5.7 and 5.8 that $(N', M_0'; R')$ is bounded and conservative. Similarly, for $(N'', M_0''; R'')$ where $R_F = \{r_4\}$, r_4 satisfies the cycle-inclusion property, and hence every R-siphon would never become empty. According to Properties 5.4 and 5.5, $(N'', M_0''; R'')$ is live and reversible. It also follows from Properties 5.7 and 5.8 that $(N'', M_0''; R')$ is bounded and conservative.

Consider the final integrated augmented marked graph $(N, M_0; R)$, shown in Fig. 6.2. For $(N, M_0; R)$, which is obtained by composing $(N', M_0'; R')$ and $(N'',$ $M_0''; R'')$ where $R_F = \{r_1, r_3,\}$, both r_1 and r_3 satisfy the cycle-inclusion property and hence, every R_F-siphon would never become empty. According to Properties 5.4 and 5.5, $(N, M_0; R)$ is live and reversible. It follows from Properties 5.7 and 5.8 that $(N, M_0; R)$ is bounded and conservative.

$(N, M_0; R)$ is a proper augmented marked graph, According to Property 4.9, $(N, M_0; R)$ is both T-coverable and P-coverable.

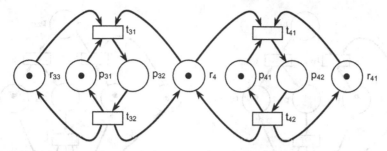

Fig. 6.6 The integrated augmented marked graph $(N'', M_0''; R'')$ obtained by composing $(N_3, M_{30}; R_3)$ and $(N_4, M_{40}; R_4)$ in Fig. 6.4

Example 6.4 Consider the dining philosophers problem (version 2). Let us regard each philosopher as a component. For philosopher H_1, the process for H_1 to grasp the chopsticks to get the food is modelled as an augmented marked graph $(N_1, M_{10}; R_1)$, where $R_1 = \{r_1, r_4\}$. Likewise, for other philosophers, we have augmented marked graphs $(N_2, M_{20}; R_2)$, $(N_3, M_{30}; R_3)$ and $(N_4, M_{40}; R_4)$, where $R_2 = \{r_1, r_2\}$, $R_3 = \{r_2, r_3\}$ and $R_4 = \{r_3, r_4\}$. Figure 6.7 shows the augmented marked graphs, while Tables 6.7 and 6.8 state the semantic meanings of places and transitions, respectively.

For $(N_1, M_{10}; R_1)$, $(N_2, M_{20}; R_2)$, $(N_3, M_{30}; R_3)$ and $(N_4, M_{40}; R_4)$, $r_{11} \in R_1$ and $r_{41} \in R_4$ refer to the same resource C_1. Likewise, $r_{12} \in R_1$ and $r_{22} \in R_2$ refer to C_2, $r_{23} \in R_2$ and $r_{33} \subset R_3$ refer to C_3, and $r_{34} \in R_3$ and $r_{44} \in R_4$ refer to C_4. Figure 6.8 shows the integrated augmented marked graph $(N', M_0'; R')$ obtained by composing $(N_1, M_{10}; R_1)$ and $(N_2, M_{20}; R_2)$ via $\{(r_{12}, r_{22})\}$. Figure 6.9 shows the integrated augmented marked graph $(N'', M_0''; R'')$ obtained by composing $(N_3, M_{30}; R_3)$ and $(N_4, M_{40}; R_4)$ via $\{(r_{34}, r_{44})\}$. $(N', M_0'; R')$ and $(N'', M_0''; R'')$ are then composed via $\{(r_{11}, r_{41}), (r_{23}, r_{33})\}$. The final integrated augmented marked graph $(N, M_0; R)$, as shown in Fig. 6.3, is obtained. As illustrated in Example 6.2, $(N, M_0; R)$ is neither live nor reversible, but bounded and conservative.

Let us investigate the system properties, based on the preservation of properties in the composition of augmented marked graphs. Each $(N_i, M_{i0}; r_i)$ is a proper augmented marked graph. According to Properties 4.1 and 4.3, each $(N_i, M_{i0}; r_i)$ is live, bounded and conservative.

Consider the integrated augmented marked graphs $(N', M_0'; R')$ and $(N'', M_0''; R'')$, shown in Figs. 6.8 and 6.9 respectively. For $(N', M_0'; R')$ where $R_F = \{r_2\}$, r_2 satisfies the cycle-inclusion property, and hence every R-siphon would never become empty. According to Properties 5.4 and 5.5, $(N', M_0'; R')$ is live and reversible. It follows from Properties 5.7 and 5.8 that $(N', M_0'; R')$ is bounded and conservative. Similarly, for $(N'', M_0''; R'')$ where $R_F = \{r_4\}$, r_4 satisfies the cycle-inclusion property, and hence every R-siphon would never become empty. According to Properties 5.4 and 5.5, $(N'', M_0''; R'')$ is live and reversible. It also follows from Properties 5.7 and 5.8 that $(N'', M_0''; R')$ is bounded and conservative.

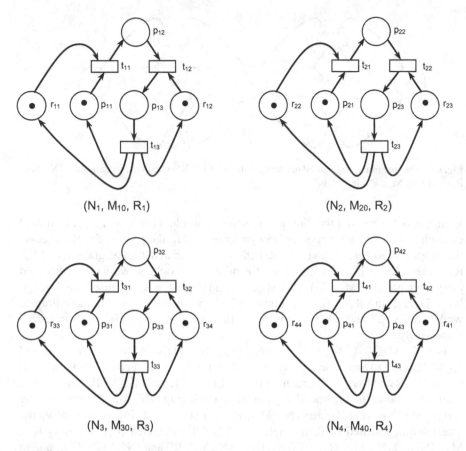

Fig. 6.7 Augmented marked graphs $(N_1, M_{10}; R_1)$, $(N_2, M_{20}; R_2)$, $(N_3, M_{30}; R_3)$ and $(N_4, M_{40}; R_4)$ representing components of the dining philosophers problem (version 2)

Consider the final integrated augmented marked graph $(N, M_0; R)$, shown in Fig. 6.3. For $(N, M_0; R)$, which is obtained by composing $(N', M_0'; R')$ and $(N'', M_0''; R'')$ where $R_F = \{r_1, r_3\}$, there exists a R_F-siphon $S = \{r_1, p_{13}, r_2, p_{23}, r_3, p_{33}, r_4, p_{43}\}$, which would become empty after firing $\langle t_{11}, t_{12}, t_{13}, t_{14} \rangle$. According to Property 5.4, $(N, M_0; R)$ is neither live nor reversible. On the other hand, according to Properties 5.7 and 5.8, $(N, M_0; R)$ is bounded and conservative.

$(N, M_0; R)$ is a proper augmented marked graph, According to Property 4.9, $(N, M_0; R)$ is both T-coverable and P-coverable.

Property-preserving composition of augmented marked graphs can be used for modelling and analysis of shared-resource systems which are synthesized from a set of processes, components, modules or subsystems. By modelling the processes, components, modules or subsystems as individual augmented marked graphs, the properties of the integrated system can be derived. Moreover, augmented marked graphs (especially, the proper augmented marked graphs) possess many desirable

Table 6.7 Semantic meanings of the places in the augmented marked graphs shown in Fig. 6.7

Place	Semantic meaning when marked
p_{11}	H_1 is meditating
p_{12}	H_1 has C_1 and prepares to pick C_2
p_{13}	H_1 has C_1 and C_2 and takes the food
p_{21}	H_2 is meditating
p_{22}	H_2 has C_2 and prepares to pick C_3
p_{23}	H_2 has C_2 and C_3 and takes the food
p_{31}	H_3 is meditating
p_{32}	H_3 has C_3 and prepares to pick C_4
p_{33}	H_3 has C_3 and C_4 and takes the food
p_{41}	H_4 is meditating
p_{42}	H_4 has C_4 and prepares to pick C_1
p_{43}	H_4 has C_4 and C_1 and takes the food
r_{11}	C_1 is available
r_{12}	C_2 is available
r_{22}	C_2 is available
r_{23}	C_3 is available
r_{33}	C_3 is available
r_{34}	C_4 is available
r_{41}	C_1 is available
r_{44}	C_4 is available

Table 6.8 Semantic meanings of the transitions in the augmented marked graphs shown in Fig. 6.7

Transition	Semantic meaning when fired
t_{11}	H_1 takes the action to grasp C_1
t_{12}	H_1 takes the action to grasp C_2
t_{13}	H_1 takes the action to return C_1 and C_2
t_{21}	H_2 takes the action to grasp C_2
t_{22}	H_2 takes the action to grasp C_3
t_{23}	H_2 takes the action to return C_2 and C_3
t_{31}	H_3 takes the action to grasp C_3
t_{32}	H_3 takes the action to grasp C_4
t_{33}	H_3 takes the action to return C_3 and C_4
t_{41}	H_4 takes the action to grasp C_4
t_{42}	H_4 takes the action to grasp C_1
t_{43}	H_4 takes the action to return C_4 and C_1

properties pertaining liveness, boundedness, reversibility and conservativeness. With the desirable properties of augmented marked graphs as well as the beauty of property-preserving composition of augmented marked graphs, a system can be effectively modelled and analyzed.

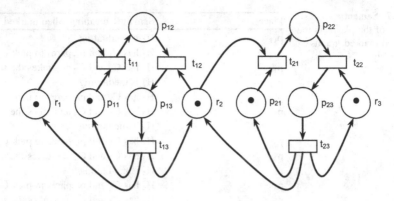

Fig. 6.8 The integrated augmented marked graph $(N', M_0'; R')$ obtained by composing $(N_1, M_{10}; R_1)$ and $(N_2, M_{20}; R_2)$ in Fig. 6.7

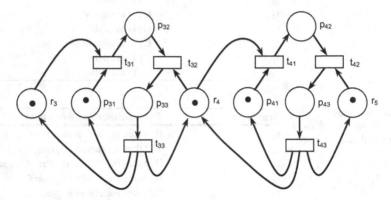

Fig. 6.9 The integrated augmented marked graph $(N'', M_0''; R'')$ obtained by composing $(N_3, M_{30}; R_3)$ and $(N_4, M_{40}; R_4)$ in Fig. 6.7

References

1. E.W. Dijkstra, Cooperating sequential processes, in *Programming Languages*, ed. by F. Genuys (Academic, London, 1965)
2. K.S. Cheung, Augmented marked graphs. Informatica **32**(1), 85–94 (2008)
3. K.S. Cheung, Augmented marked graphs and the analysis of shared resource systems, in *Petri Net: Theory and Application*, ed. by V. Kordic (I-Tech Publishing, Vienna, 2008), pp. 377–400
4. K.S. Cheung, A synthesis method for designing shared-resource systems. Comput. Inform. **24** (6), 629–653 (2005)
5. K.S. Cheung, A formal method for synthesising components of shared resource systems. Int. J. Comput. Syst. Sci. Eng. **22**(6), 349–358 (2007)

Part III
Application to System Integration

Chapter 7
Component-Based System Integration

This chapter describes how the theories of augmented marked graphs described in the previous chapters can be effectively applied to system integration. It starts with introducing component-based system design, where the challenges in system integration are discussed. We show how augmented marked graphs can be used for modelling the components of a system. Then, we show how these augmented marked graphs can be composed as an integrated system whose properties can be effectively analyzed.

7.1 Component-Based System Design

Among other system design methodologies, component-based system design is a promising methodology that emphasizes two key concepts—the compositional synthesis of a system from components or modules, and the maximal reuse of the components. In component-based system design, a system is considered as the integrated whole of a set of interacting or inter-related components [1–4]. Each component is basically a building block which is self-contained and encapsulated with functions and processes.

From the structural perspective, a component-based system possesses a static structure which delineates how its components are structurally organized, associated, inter-related or inter-depended. From the behavioural perspective, a component-based system exhibits a collection of behavioural patterns, each delineating a scenario in which the inter-related components interact with each other for some functional purposes. Typically, the system design process begins with identifying and defining the components. An integrated system is then obtained by composing or integrating these components.

In component-based system design, it is important for the system designer to ensure correctness of the integrated system. This correctness, usually called design correctness, means that the system should be free from erroneous situations such as deadlock and capacity overflow. For a system with distributed components,

K.S. Cheung, *Augmented Marked Graphs*, DOI 10.1007/978-3-319-06428-4_7,
© Springer International Publishing Switzerland 2014

deadlocks occur when two or more components are each waiting for the other to finish, and thus neither ever does. These components are usually competing for some common resources. Capacity overflow is another erroneous situation, where the capacity of a component exceeds its defined limit, for example, a memory exceeds its capacity limit. There are also other erroneous situations. For example, a system cannot be reinitialized, meaning that the home state of a system cannot be reached from a particular state of execution.

In reality, computer systems and automated systems are usually large and complex. A system may have many components or modules. Therefore, in component-based system design, it is a difficult challenge for the system designer to ensure that the integrated system is free from erroneous situations. The system designer should first ensure that every individual component of the system is correct in the sense that it is live, bounded and reversible. Then, all the possible interactions and collaborations among the inter-related components should be carefully walked through, in order to check if any possible erroneous situation would occur. The process is very time-consuming.

System integration is an essential step in component-based system design, where an integrated system is synthesized from the components. It is important to highlight that the design correctness of the individual components does not guarantee that the integrated system would be correct. Erroneous situations may occur, especially when there involves concurrency and competition of shared resources among the components. In technical terminology, the integrated system may not be live, bounded and reversible even if all the components are live, bounded and reversible, meaning that the properties of the components may not be preserved after the composition.

To tackle the challenges in system integration, formal and mathematically sound techniques are essentially required in modelling the components and analyzing the properties of the integrated system. Augmented marked graphs can be effectively used for this purpose [5–8]. The previous chapters present the theories pertaining to augmented marked graphs and the property-preserving composition of augmented marked graphs. In this chapter, we show how augmented marked graphs or proper augmented marked graphs can be used for modelling the components of a system. Based on the properties of augmented marked graphs, the system designer can check the liveness, boundedness, reversibility and conservativeness of the components. Then, it follows from the property-preserving composition of augmented marked graphs to determine whether the integrated system is live, bounded, reversible and conservative.

7.2 Modelling and Analysis Using Augmented Marked Graphs

This section describes the modelling and analysis of component-based systems using augmented marked graphs. We outline the modelling, integration and analysis process as follows.

Step 1.   Modelling the components as augmented marked graphs.
Suppose that a set of components $C_1, C_2, \ldots, C_n$ are identified. For each C_i, specify the behavioural pattern of C_i as a proper augmented marked graph $(N_i, M_{i0}; R_i)$, where R_i represents the common resources to be used by C_i.

Step 2.   Composing the components as an integrated system.
Obtained an integrated augmented marked graph $(N, M_0; R)$ by composing $(N_1, M_{10}; R_1), (N_2, M_{20}; R_2), \ldots, (N_n, M_{n0}; R_n)$ via their common resource places.

Step 3.   Analyzing the properties of the individual components.
Based on the theories in Chaps. 3 and 4, check the liveness, boundedness, reversibility and conservativeness of each component represented by $(N_i, M_{i0}; R_i)$.

Step 4.   Analyzing the properties of the integrated system.
Based on the theories in Chap. 5, check the liveness, boundedness, reversibility and conservativeness of the integrated system represented by $(N, M_0; R)$.
It would then be concluded whether the integrated system is live, bounded, reversibile and conservative.

7.3   Examples for Illustration

In the following, we present two examples to illustrate the modelling, integration and analysis of component-based systems using augmented marked graphs.

Example 7.1 Let us consider a component-based system consisting of four components, namely, C_1, C_2, C_3 and C_4. There components exhibit some concurrent and asynchronous processes. There are six pieces of common resources, namely, S_1, S_2, S_3, S_4, S_5 and S_6. These common resources are shared among the components. Figure 7.1 outlines the component-based system.
   Each component exhibits some sequences of activities or operations, in which common resources may be occupied. The behavioural patterns of the components are briefly described as follows.

Component C_1   At its initial idle state, C_1 invokes operation o_{11} only if S_1 is available. While o_{11} is being processed, S_1 is occupied. Once o_{11} finishes processing, operation o_{12} is invoked only if S_2 is available. S_1 is then released. While o_{12} is being processed, S_2 is occupied. Once o_{12} finishes processing, S_2 is released and C_1 returns to its idle state. From time to time, S_1 is occupied upon receipt of signal m_{11} and released upon receipt of signal m_{12}. Similarly, S_2 is occupied upon receipt of signal m_{13} and released upon receipt of signal m_{14}.

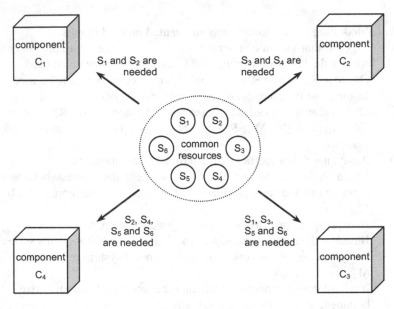

Fig. 7.1 A component-based system with common resources

Component C_2 At its initial idle state, C_2 invokes operation o_{21} only if S_3 is available. While o_{21} is being processed, S_3 is occupied. Once o_{21} finishes processing, operation o_{22} is invoked only if S_4 is available. S_3 is then released. While o_{22} is being processed, S_4 is occupied. Once o_{22} finishes processing, S_4 is released and C_2 returns to its idle state. From time to time, S_3 is occupied upon receipt of signal m_{21} and released upon receipt of signal m_{22}. Similarly, S_4 is occupied upon receipt of signal m_{23} and released upon receipt of signal m_{24}.

Component C_3 At its initial idle state, C_3 may invoke operation o_{31} only if S_1, S_3, S_5 and S_6 are available. While o_{31} is being processed, S_1, S_3, S_5 and S_6 are occupied. Once o_{31} finishes processing, S_1, S_3, S_5 and S_6 are released and C_3 returns to its idle state.

Component C_4 At its initial idle state, C_4 may invoke operation o_{41} only if S_2, S_4, S_5 and S_6 are available. While o_{41} is being processed, S_2, S_4, S_5 and S_6 are occupied. Once o_{41} finishes processing, S_2, S_4, S_5 and S_6 are released and C_4 returns to its idle state.

Let us start with representing each component as an augmented marked graph. The event occurrences involved in the component as well as their pre-conditions and post-conditions are first identified. For each event occurrence, a transition is created for denoting the location of occurrence. Input and output places are then created to denote the locations of its pre-conditions and post-conditions. An initial marking is created to denote the system initial state. Execution for the component begins at this initial marking which semantically means its initial idle state, and ends at the same marking.

Component C_1 is specified as augmented marked graph $(N_1, M_{10}; R_1)$, where $R_1 = \{ r_{11}, r_{12} \}$. C_2 is specified as $(N_2, M_{20}; R_2)$, where $R_2 = \{ r_{23}, r_{24} \}$. C_3 is specified as $(N_3, M_{30}; R_3)$, where $R_3 = \{ r_{31}, r_{33}, r_{35}, r_{36} \}$. C_4 is specified as $(N_4, M_{40}; R_4)$, where $R_4 = \{ r_{42}, r_{44}, r_{45}, r_{46} \}$. They are shown in Fig. 7.2 while Tables 7.1 and 7.2 state the semantic meanings of places and transitions, respectively.

The common resources S_1, S_2, S_3, S_4, S_5 and S_6 are represented by the resources places in the augmented marked graphs. For $(N_1, M_{10}; R_1)$, $(N_2, M_{20}; R_2)$, $(N_3, M_{30}; R_3)$ and $(N_4, M_{40}; R_4)$, $r_{11} \in R_1$ and $r_{31} \in R_3$ refer to the same resource S_1. Likewise, $r_{12} \in R_1$ and $r_{42} \in R_4$ refer to S_2, $r_{23} \in R_2$ and $r_{33} \in R_3$ refer to S_3, $r_{24} \in R_2$ and $r_{44} \in R_4$ refer to S_4, $r_{35} \in R_3$ and $r_{45} \in R_4$ refer S_5, and $r_{36} \in R_3$ and $r_{46} \in R_4$ refer to S_6. $(N_1, M_{10}; R_1)$, $(N_2, M_{20}; R_2)$, $(N_3, M_{30}; R_3)$ and $(N_4, M_{40}; R_4)$ are to be composed via these common resource places.

The next step is to synthesis the integrated system by composing these augmented marked graphs via their common resource places. Figure 7.3 shows the integrated augmented marked graph $(N', M_0'; R')$ obtained by composing $(N_1, M_{10}; R_1)$ and $(N_3, M_{30}; R_3)$ via $\{ (r_{11}, r_{31}) \}$. For $(N', M_0'; R')$ where $R' = \{ r_1, r_{12}, r_{33}, r_{35}, r_{36} \}$, r_1 is the place obtained after fusing r_{11} and r_{31}. Figure 7.4 shows the integrated augmented marked graph $(N'', M_0''; R'')$ obtained by composing $(N_2, M_{20}; R_2)$ and $(N_4, M_{40}; R_4)$ via $\{ (r_{24}, r_{44}) \}$. For $(N'', M_0''; R'')$ where $R'' = \{ r_4, r_{23}, r_{42}, r_{45}, r_{46} \}$, r_4 is the place obtained after fusing r_{24} and r_{44}.

Figure 7.5 then shows the final integrated augmented marked graph $(N, M_0; R)$ obtained by composing $(N', M_0'; R')$ and $(N'', M_0''; R'')$ via $\{ (r_{12}, r_{42}), (r_{33}, r_{23}), (r_{35}, r_{45}), (r_{36}, r_{46}) \}$, while Tables 7.3 and 7.4 state the semantic meanings of places and transitions, respectively. For $(N, M_0; R)$ where $R = \{ r_1, r_2, r_3, r_4, r_5, r_6 \}$, where r_2 is the place obtained after fusing r_{12} and r_{42}, r_3 is the place obtained after fusing r_{33} and r_{23}, r_5 is the place obtained after fusing r_{35} and r_{45}, and r_6 is the place obtained after fusing r_{36} and r_{46}.

Let us first analyze the properties of the components. Consider $(N_1, M_{10}; R_1)$. The siphon-trap property is satisfied, and every siphon would never become empty. According to Properties 3.11 and 3.12, $(N_1, M_{10}; R_1)$ is live and reversible. We may also analyse the liveness and reversibility of $(N_1, M_{10}; R_1)$ based on cycle-inclusion property. For $(N_1, M_{10}; R_1)$, every place in R_1 satisfies the cycle-inclusion property. According to property 3.16, $(N_1, M_{10}; R_1)$ is live and reversible. Similarly, $(N_2, M_{20}; R_2)$, $(N_3, M_{30}; R_3)$ and $(N_4, M_{40}; R_4)$ are live and reversible. Besides, $(N_1, M_{10}; R_1)$, $(N_2, M_{20}; R_2)$, $(N_3, M_{30}; R_3)$ and $(N_4, M_{40}; R_4)$ are proper augmented marked graphs. According to Property 4.3, $(N_1, M_{10}; R_1)$, $(N_2, M_{20}; R_2)$, $(N_3, M_{30}; R_3)$ and $(N_4, M_{40}; R_4)$ are bounded and conservative.

Consider $(N', M_0'; R')$ which is obtained by composing $(N_1, M_{10}; R_1)$ and $(N_3, M_{30}; R_3)$. Since $(N_1, M_{10}; R_1)$ and $(N_3, M_{30}; R_3)$ are bounded and conservative,

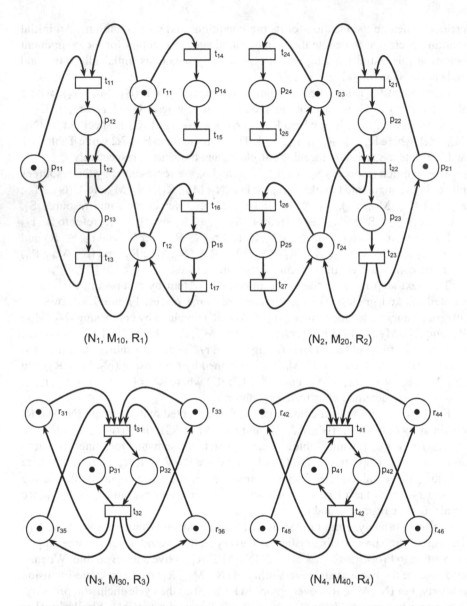

Fig. 7.2 Modelling of components as augmented marked graphs $(N_1, M_{10}; R_1)$, $(N_2, M_{20}; R_2)$, $(N_3, M_{30}; R_3)$ and $(N_4, M_{40}; R_4)$

according to Properties 5.7 and 5.8, $(N', M_0'; R')$ is bounded and conservative. For $(N', M_0'; R')$ where $R_F = \{\ r_1\ \}$ is the set of fused places, r_1 satisfies the cycle-inclusion property, and hence, every R_F-siphon would never become empty. According to Property 5.4, $(N', M_0'; R')$ is live and reversible.

Table 7.1 Semantic meanings of the places in the augmented marked graphs shown in Fig. 7.2

Place	Semantic meaning
p_{11}	C_1 is at the idle state
p_{12}	C_1 is performing operation o_{11}, where S_1 is occupied
p_{13}	C_1 is performing operation o_{12}, where S_2 is occupied
p_{14}	S_1 is occupied
p_{15}	S_2 is occupied
p_{21}	C_2 is at the idle state
p_{22}	C_2 is performing operation o_{21}, where S_3 is occupied
p_{23}	C_2 is performing operation o_{22}, where S_4 is occupied
p_{24}	S_3 is occupied
p_{25}	S_4 is occupied
p_{31}	C_3 is at the idle state
p_{32}	C_3 is performing operation o_{31}, where S_1, S_3, S_5 and S_6 are occupied
p_{41}	C_4 is at the idle state
p_{42}	C_4 is performing operation o_{41}, where S_2, S_4, S_5 and S_6 are occupied
r_{11}	S_1 is available
r_{12}	S_2 is available
r_{23}	S_3 is available
r_{24}	S_4 is available
r_{31}	S_1 is available
r_{33}	S_3 is available
r_{35}	S_5 is available
r_{36}	S_6 is available
r_{42}	S_2 is available
r_{44}	S_4 is available
r_{45}	S_5 is available
r_{46}	S_6 is available

Table 7.2 Semantic meanings of the transitions in the augmented marked graphs in Fig. 7.2

Transition	Semantic meaning
t_{11}	C_1 starts operation o_{11}
t_{12}	C_1 finishes operation o_{11} and starts operation o_{12}
t_{13}	C_1 finishes operation o_{12}
t_{14}	C_1 receives signal m_{11}
t_{15}	C_1 receives signal m_{12}
t_{16}	C_1 receives signal m_{13}
t_{17}	C_1 receives signal m_{14}
t_{21}	C_2 starts operation o_{21}
t_{22}	C_2 finishes operation o_{21} and starts operation o_{22}
t_{23}	C_2 finishes operation o_{22}
t_{24}	C_2 receives signal m_{21}
t_{25}	C_2 receives signal m_{22}
t_{26}	C_2 receives signal m_{23}
t_{27}	C_2 receives signal m_{24}
t_{31}	C_3 starts operation o_{31}
t_{32}	C_3 finishes operation o_{31}
t_{41}	C_4 starts operation o_{41}
t_{42}	C_4 finishes operation o_{41}

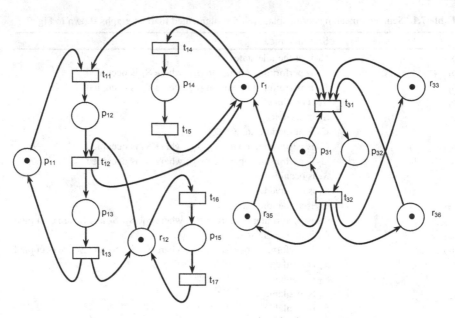

Fig. 7.3 The integrated augmented marked graphs $(N', M_0'; R')$ obtained by composing $(N_1, M_{10}; R_1)$ and $(N_3, M_{30}; R_3)$ in Fig. 7.2

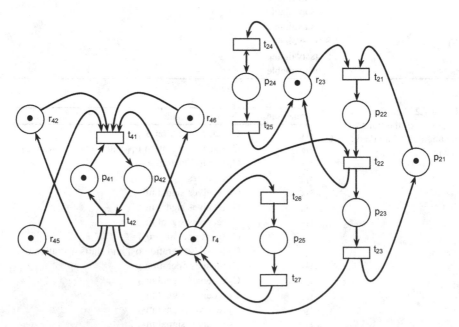

Fig. 7.4 The integrated augmented marked graphs $(N'', M_0''; R'')$ obtained by composing $(N_2, M_{20}; R_2)$ and $(N_4, M_{40}; R_4)$ in Fig. 7.2

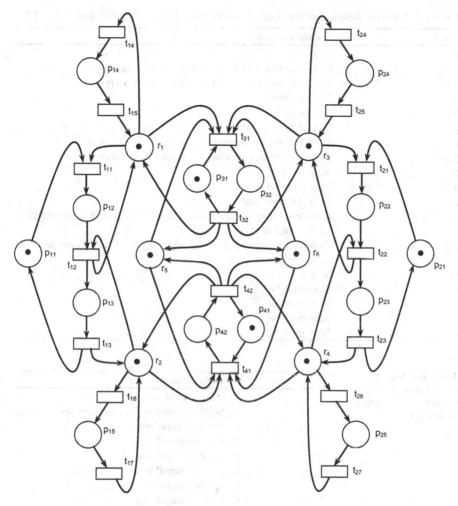

Fig. 7.5 The final integrated augmented marked graphs $(N, M_0; R)$ obtained by composing $(N', M_0'; R')$ and $(N'', M_0''; R'')$ in Figs. 7.3 and 7.4

Next, consider $(N'', M_0''; R'')$ which is obtained by composing $(N_2, M_{20}; R_2)$ and $(N_4, M_{40}; R_4)$. Since $(N_2, M_{20}; R_2)$ and $(N_4, M_{40}; R_4)$ are bounded and conservative, according to Properties 5.7 and 5.8, $(N'', M_0''; R'')$ is bounded and conservative. For $(N'', M_0''; R'')$ where $R_F = \{ r_4 \}$ is the set of fused places, r_4 satisfies the cycle-inclusion property, and hence, every R_F-siphon would never become empty. According to Properties 5.4 and 5.5, $(N'', M_0''; R'')$ is live and reversible.

Table 7.3 Semantic meanings of the places in the augmented marked graph shown in Fig. 7.5

Place	Semantic meaning
p_{11}	C_1 is at the idle state
p_{12}	C_1 is performing operation o_{11}, where S_1 is occupied
p_{13}	C_1 is performing operation o_{12}, where S_2 is occupied
p_{14}	S_1 is occupied
p_{15}	S_2 is occupied
p_{21}	C_2 is at the idle state
p_{22}	C_2 is performing operation o_{21}, where S_3 is occupied
p_{23}	C_2 is performing operation o_{22}, where S_4 is occupied
p_{24}	S_3 is occupied
p_{25}	S_4 is occupied
p_{31}	C_3 is at the idle state
p_{32}	C_3 is performing operation o_{31}, where S_1, S_3, S_5 and S_6 are occupied
p_{41}	C_4 is at the idle state
p_{42}	C_4 is performing operation o_{41}, where S_2, S_4, S_5 and S_6 are occupied
r_1	S_1 is available
r_2	S_2 is available
r_3	S_3 is available
r_4	S_4 is available
r_5	S_5 is available
r_6	S_6 is available

Table 7.4 Semantic meanings of the transitions in the augmented marked graph shown in Fig. 7.5

Transition	Semantic meaning
t_{11}	C_1 starts operation o_{11}
t_{12}	C_1 finishes operation o_{11} and starts operation o_{12}
t_{13}	C_1 finishes operation o_{12}
t_{14}	C_1 receives signal m_{11}
t_{15}	C_1 receives signal m_{12}
t_{16}	C_1 receives signal m_{13}
t_{17}	C_1 receives signal m_{14}
t_{21}	C_2 starts operation o_{21}
t_{22}	C_2 finishes operation o_{21} and starts operation o_{22}
t_{23}	C_2 finishes operation o_{22}
t_{24}	C_2 receives signal m_{21}
t_{25}	C_2 receives signal m_{22}
t_{26}	C_2 receives signal m_{23}
t_{27}	C_2 receives signal m_{24}
t_{31}	C_3 starts operation o_{31}
t_{32}	C_3 finishes operation o_{31}
t_{41}	C_4 starts operation o_{41}
t_{42}	C_4 finishes operation o_{41}

Both the integrated augmented marked graphs $(N', M_0'; R')$ and $(N'', M_0''; R'')$ are proven to be live, bounded, reversible and conservative. Now, let us consider the final integrated augmented marked graph $(N, M_0; R)$ obtained by composing $(N', M_0'; R')$ and $(N'', M_0''; R'')$. Since $(N', M_0'; R')$ and $(N'', M_0''; R'')$ are bounded and conservative, according to Properties 5.7 and 5.8, $(N, M_0; R)$ is bounded and conservative. For $(N, M_0; R)$ where $R_F = \{ r_2, r_3, r_5, r_6 \}$, the places r_2, r_3, r_5 and r_6 satisfy the cycle-inclusion property, and hence, every R_F-siphon would never become empty. According to Properties 5.4 and 5.5, $(N, M_0; R)$ is live and reversible.

It may be concluded that the integrated system is live, bounded, reversible and conservative.

Example 7.2 It is a revised version of Example 7.1. The component-based system consists of four components, C_1, C_2, C_3 and C_4, sharing six pieces of common resources, S_1, S_2, S_3, S_4, S_5 and S_6, as shown in Fig. 7.1. Each component exhibits some sequences of activities or operations, in which common resources may be occupied. In this revised version, the behavioural patterns of the components are briefly described as follows.

Component C_1   At its initial idle state, C_1 invokes operation o_{11} only if S_1 is available. While o_{11} is being processed, S_1 is occupied. Once o_{11} finishes processing, operation o_{12} is invoked only if S_2 is available. S_1 is then released. While o_{12} is being processed, S_2 is occupied. Once o_{12} finishes processing, S_2 is released and C_1 returns to its idle state. From time to time, S_1 is occupied upon receipt of signal m_{11} and released upon receipt of signal m_{12}. Similarly, S_2 is withheld upon receipt of signal m_{13} and occupied upon receipt of signal m_{14}.

Component C_2   At its initial idle state, C_2 invokes operation o_{21} only if S_3 is available. While o_{21} is being processed, S_3 is occupied. Once o_{21} finishes processing, operation o_{22} is invoked only if S_4 is available. S_3 is then released. While o_{22} is being processed, S_4 is occupied. Once o_{22} finishes processing, S_4 is released and C_2 returns to its idle state. From time to time, S_3 is occupied upon receipt of signal m_{21} and released upon receipt of signal m_{22}. Similarly S_4 is withheld upon receipt of signal m_{23} and occupied upon receipt of signal m_{24}.

Component C_3   At its initial idle state, C_3 may invoke operation o_{31} only if S_1, and S_5 are available. While o_{31} is being processed, S_1, S_3 and S_5 are occupied. Once o_{31} finishes processing, operation o_{32} is invoked only if S_6 is also available. While operation o_{32} is being processed, S_1, S_3, S_5 and S_6 are occupied. Once o_{32} finishes processing, S_1, S_3, S_5 and S_6 are released and C_3 returns to its idle state.

Component C_4   At its initial idle state, C_4 may invoke operation o_{41} only if S_2, and S_6 are available. While o_{41} is being processed, S_2, S_4 and S_6 are occupied. Once o_{41} finishes processing, operation o_{42} is involved only if S_5 is also available. While operation o_{42} is being processed, S_2, S_4, S_5 and S_6 are occupied. Once o_{42} finishes processing, S_2, S_4, S_5 and S_6 are released and C_4 returns to its idle state.

Component C_1 is specified as augmented marked graph $(N_1, M_{10}; R_1)$, where $R_1 = \{ r_{11}, r_{12} \}$. C_2 is specified as $(N_2, M_{20}; R_2)$, where $R_2 = \{ r_{23}, r_{24} \}$. C_3 is specified as $(N_3, M_{30}; R_3)$, where $R_3 = \{ r_{31}, r_{33}, r_{35}, r_{36} \}$. C_4 is specified as $(N_4, M_{40}; R_4)$, where $R_4 = \{ r_{42}, r_{44}, r_{45}, r_{46} \}$. They are shown in Fig. 7.6, while Tables 7.5 and 7.6 state the semantic meanings of places and transitions, respectively.

Similar to Example 7.1, the common resources S_1, S_2, S_3, S_4, S_5 and S_6 are represented by the resources places in the augmented marked graphs. For $(N_1, M_{10}; R_1)$, $(N_2, M_{20}; R_2)$, $(N_3, M_{30}; R_3)$ and $(N_4, M_{40}; R_4)$, $r_{11} \in R_1$ and $r_{31} \in R_3$ refer to the same resource S_1. Likewise, $r_{12} \in R_1$ and $r_{42} \in R_4$ refer to S_2, $r_{23} \in R_2$ and $r_{33} \in R_3$ refer to S_3, $r_{24} \in R_2$ and $r_{44} \in R_4$ refer to S_4. $r_{35} \in R_3$ and $r_{45} \in R_4$ refer to S_5, and $r_{36} \in R_3$ and $r_{46} \in R_4$ refer to the same resource S_6. $(N_1, M_{10}; R_1)$, $(N_2, M_{20}; R_2)$, $(N_3, M_{30}; R_3)$ and $(N_4, M_{40}; R_4)$ are to be composed via these common resource places.

The next step is to synthesis the integrated system by composing these augmented marked graphs via their common resource places. Figure 7.7 shows the integrated augmented marked graph $(N', M_0'; R')$ obtained by composing $(N_1, M_{10}; R_1)$ and $(N_3, M_{30}; R_3)$ via $\{ (r_{11}, r_{31}) \}$. For $(N', M_0'; R')$ where $R' = \{ r_1, r_{12}, r_{33}, r_{35}, r_{36} \}$, r_1 is the place obtained after fusing r_{11} and r_{31}. Figure 7.8 shows the integrated augmented marked graph $(N'', M_0''; R'')$ obtained by composing $(N_2, M_{20}; R_2)$ and $(N_4, M_{40}; R_4)$ via $\{ (r_{24}, r_{44}) \}$. For $(N'', M_0''; R'')$ where $R'' = \{ r_4, r_{23}, r_{42}, r_{45}, r_{46} \}$, r_4 is the place obtained after fusing r_{24} and r_{44}.

Figure 7.9 then shows the final integrated augmented marked graph $(N, M_0; R)$ obtained by composing $(N', M_0'; R')$ and $(N'', M_0''; R'')$ via $\{ (r_{12}, r_{42}), (r_{33}, r_{23}), (r_{35}, r_{45}), (r_{36}, r_{46}) \}$, while Tables 7.7 and 7.8 state the semantic meanings of places and transitions, respectively. For $(N, M_0; R)$ where $R = \{ r_1, r_2, r_3, r_4, r_5, r_6 \}$, where r_2 is the place obtained after fusing r_{12} and r_{42}, r_3 is the place obtained after fusing r_{33} and r_{23}, r_5 is the place obtained after fusing r_{35} and r_{45}, and r_6 is the place obtained after fusing r_{36} and r_{46}.

Let us first analyze the properties of the components. Consider $(N_1, M_{10}; R_1)$. The siphon-trap property is satisfied, and every siphon would never become empty. According to Properties 3.11 and 3.12, $(N_1, M_{10}; R_1)$ is live and reversible. We may also analyse the liveness and reversibility of $(N_1, M_{10}; R_1)$ based on cycle-inclusion

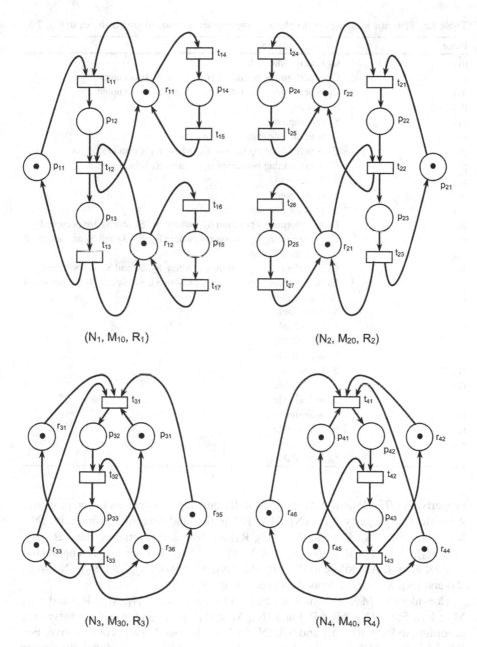

Fig. 7.6 Modelling of components as augmented marked graphs $(N_1, M_{10}; R_1)$, $(N_2, M_{20}; R_2)$, $(N_3, M_{30}; R_3)$ and $(N_4, M_{40}; R_4)$

Table 7.5 Semantic meanings of the places in the augmented marked graphs shown in Fig. 7.6

Place	Semantic meaning
p_{11}	C_1 is at the idle state
p_{12}	C_1 is performing operation o_{11}, where S_1 is occupied
p_{13}	C_1 is performing operation o_{12}, where S_2 is occupied
p_{14}	S_1 is occupied
p_{15}	S_2 is occupied
p_{21}	C_2 is at the idle state
p_{22}	C_2 is performing operation o_{21}, where S_3 is occupied
p_{23}	C_2 is performing operation o_{22}, where S_4 is occupied
p_{24}	S_3 is occupied
p_{25}	S_4 is occupied
p_{31}	C_3 is at the idle state
p_{32}	C_3 is performing operation o_{31}, where S_1, S_3 and S_5 are occupied
p_{33}	C_3 is performing operation o_{32}, where S_1, S_3, S_5 and S_6 are occupied
p_{41}	C_4 is at the idle state
p_{42}	C_4 is performing operation o_{41}, where S_2, S_4 and S_6 are occupied
p_{43}	C_4 is performing operation o_{42}, where S_2, S_4, S_5 and S_5 are occupied
r_{11}	S_1 is available
r_{12}	S_2 is available
r_{23}	S_3 is available
r_{24}	S_4 is available
r_{31}	S_1 is available
r_{33}	S_3 is available
r_{35}	S_5 is available
r_{36}	S_6 is available
r_{42}	S_2 is available
r_{44}	S_4 is available
r_{45}	S_5 is available
r_{46}	S_6 is available

property. For $(N_1, M_{10}; R_1)$, every place in R_1 satisfies the cycle-inclusion property. According to property 3.16, $(N_1, M_{10}; R_1)$ is live and reversible. Similarly, $(N_2, M_{20}; R_2)$, $(N_3, M_{30}; R_3)$ and $(N_4, M_{40}; R_4)$ are live and reversible. Besides, $(N_1, M_{10}; R_1)$, $(N_2, M_{20}; R_2)$, $(N_3, M_{30}; R_3)$ and $(N_4, M_{40}; R_4)$ are proper augmented marked graphs. According to Property 4.3, $(N_1, M_{10}; R_1)$, $(N_2, M_{20}; R_2)$, $(N_3, M_{30}; R_3)$ and $(N_4, M_{40}; R_4)$ bounded and conservative.

Consider $(N', M_0'; R')$ which is obtained by composing $(N_1, M_{10}; R_1)$ and $(N_3, M_{30}; R_3)$. Since $(N_1, M_{10}; R_1)$ and $(N_3, M_{30}; R_3)$ are bounded and conservative, according to Properties 5.7 and 5.8, $(N', M_0'; R')$ is bounded and conservative. For $(N', M_0'; R')$ where $R_F = \{ r_1 \}$ is the set of fused places, r_1 satisfies the cycle-inclusion property, and hence, every R_F-siphon would never become empty. According to Properties 5.4 and 5.5, $(N', M_0'; R')$ is live and reversible.

Table 7.6 Semantic meanings of the transitions in the augmented marked graphs in Fig. 7.6

Transition	Semantic meaning
t_{11}	C_1 starts operation o_{11}
t_{12}	C_1 finishes operation o_{11} and starts operation o_{12}
t_{13}	C_1 finishes operation o_{12}
t_{14}	C_1 receives signal m_{11}
t_{15}	C_1 receives signal m_{12}
t_{16}	C_1 receives signal m_{13}
t_{17}	C_1 receives signal m_{14}
t_{21}	C_2 starts operation o_{21}
t_{22}	C_2 finishes operation o_{21} and starts operation o_{22}
t_{23}	C_2 finishes operation o_{22}
t_{24}	C_2 receives signal m_{21}
t_{25}	C_2 receives signal m_{22}
t_{26}	C_2 receives signal m_{23}
t_{27}	C_2 receives signal m_{24}
t_{31}	C_3 starts operation o_{31}
t_{32}	C_3 finishes operation o_{31} and starts operation o_{32}
t_{33}	C_3 finishes operation o_{32}
t_{41}	C_4 starts operation o_{41}
t_{42}	C_4 finishes operation o_{41} and starts operation o_{42}
t_{43}	C_4 finishes operation o_{42}

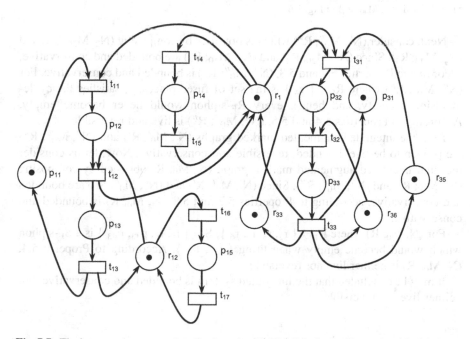

Fig. 7.7 The integrated augmented marked graphs $(N', M_0'; R')$ obtained by composing $(N_1, M_{10}; R_1)$ and $(N_3, M_{30}; R_3)$ in Fig. 7.6

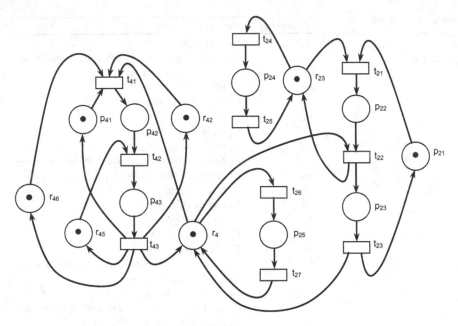

Fig. 7.8 The integrated augmented marked graphs $(N'', M_0''; R'')$ obtained by composing $(N_2, M_{20}; R_2)$ and $(N_4, M_{40}; R_4)$ in Fig. 7.6

Next, consider $(N'', M_0''; R'')$ which is obtained by composing $(N_2, M_{20}; R_2)$ and $(N_4, M_{40}; R_4)$. Since $(N_2, M_{20}; R_2)$ and $(N_4, M_{40}; R_4)$ are bounded and conservative, according to Properties 5.7 and 5.8, $(N'', M_0''; R'')$ is bounded and conservative. For $(N'', M_0''; R'')$ where $R_F = \{ r_4 \}$ is the set of fused places, r_4 satisfies the cycle-inclusion property, and hence, every R_F-siphon would never become empty. According to Properties 5.4 and 5.5, $(N'', M_0''; R'')$ is live and reversible.

Both the integrated augmented marked graphs $(N', M_0'; R')$ and $(N'', M_0''; R'')$ are proven to be live, bounded, reversible and conservative. Now, let us consider the final integrated augmented marked graph $(N, M_0; R)$ obtained by composing $(N', M_0'; R')$ and $(N'', M_0''; R'')$. Since $(N', M_0'; R')$ and $(N'', M_0''; R'')$ are bounded and conservative, according to Properties 5.7 and 5.8, $(N, M_0; R)$ is bounded and conservative.

For $(N, M_0; R)$ where $R_F = \{ r_2, r_3, r_5, r_6 \}$, $S = \{ r_5, r_6, p_{33}, p_{43} \}$ is a S_F-siphon which would become empty when firing $\langle t_{31}, t_{41} \rangle$. According to Property 5.4, $(N, M_0; R)$ is neither live nor reversible.

It may be concluded that the integrated system is bounded and conservative, but neither live nor reversible.

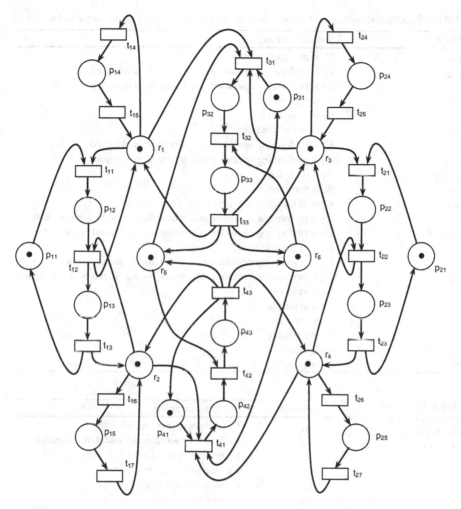

Fig. 7.9 The final integrated augmented marked graphs (N, M_0; R) obtained by composing (N′, M_0'; R′) and (N″, M_0''; R″) in Figs. 7.7 and 7.8

Table 7.7 Semantic meanings of the places in the augmented marked graph shown in Fig. 7.9

Place	Semantic meaning
p_{11}	C_1 is at the idle state
p_{12}	C_1 is performing operation o_{11}, where S_1 is occupied
p_{13}	C_1 is performing operation o_{12}, where S_2 is occupied
p_{14}	S_1 is occupied
p_{15}	S_2 is occupied
p_{21}	C_2 is at the idle state
p_{22}	C_2 is performing operation o_{21}, where S_3 is occupied
p_{23}	C_2 is performing operation o_{22}, where S_4 is occupied
p_{24}	S_3 is occupied
p_{25}	S_4 is occupied
p_{31}	C_3 is at the idle state
p_{32}	C_3 is performing operation o_{31}, where S_1, S_3 and S_5 are occupied
p_{33}	C_3 is performing operation o_{32}, where S_1, S_3, S_5 and S_6 are occupied
p_{41}	C_4 is at the idle state
p_{42}	C_4 is performing operation o_{41}, where S_2, S_4 and S_6 are occupied
p_{43}	C_4 is performing operation o_{42}, where S_2, S_4, S_5 and S_5 are occupied
r_1	S_1 is available
r_2	S_2 is available
r_3	S_3 is available
r_4	S_4 is available
r_5	S_5 is available
r_6	S_6 is available

Table 7.8 Semantic meanings of the transitions in the augmented marked graph shown in Fig. Fig. 7.9

Transition	Semantic meaning
t_{11}	C_1 starts operation o_{11}
t_{12}	C_1 finishes operation o_{11} and starts operation o_{12}
t_{13}	C_1 finishes operation o_{12}
t_{14}	C_1 receives signal m_{11}
t_{15}	C_1 receives signal m_{12}
t_{16}	C_1 receives signal m_{13}
t_{17}	C_1 receives signal m_{14}
t_{21}	C_2 starts operation o_{21}
t_{22}	C_2 finishes operation o_{21} and starts operation o_{22}
t_{23}	C_2 finishes operation o_{22}
t_{24}	C_2 receives signal m_{21}
t_{25}	C_2 receives signal m_{22}
t_{26}	C_2 receives signal m_{23}
t_{27}	C_2 receives signal m_{24}
t_{31}	C_3 starts operation o_{31}
t_{32}	C_3 finishes operation o_{31} and starts operation o_{32}
t_{33}	C_3 finishes operation o_{32}
t_{41}	C_4 starts operation o_{41}
t_{42}	C_4 finishes operation o_{41} and starts operation o_{42}
t_{43}	C_4 finishes operation o_{42}

References

1. G.T. Leavens, M. Sitaraman (eds.), *Foundations of Component-Based Systems* (Cambridge University Press, Cambridge, 2000)
2. G.T. Heineman, W.T. Councill, *Component-Based Software Engineering: Putting the Pieces Together* (Addison-Wesley, Boston, 2002)
3. C. Szyperski, *Component Software: Beyond Object-Oriented Programming* (Addison-Wesley, Reading, 2002)
4. M. Ramachandran, *Software Components: Guidelines and Applications* (Nova, New York, 2008)
5. K.S. Cheung, Compositional synthesis of distributed system components based on augmented marked graphs. J. Comput. Sci. Technol. **8**(1), 34–40 (2008)
6. K.S. Cheung, Composition of augmented marked graphs and its application to component-based system design. Inf. Technol. Control **36**(3), 310–317 (2007)
7. K.S. Cheung, A formal method for synthesising components of shared resource systems. Int. J. Comput. Syst. Sci. Eng. **22**(6), 349–358 (2007)
8. K.S. Cheung, Property-preserving composition of distributed system components, in *Advanced Parallel Processing Technologies*. Lecture Notes in Computer Science, vol. 4847 (Springer, Berlin, 2007), pp. 108–117
9. K.S. Cheung, Composition of augmented marked graphs and its application to system integration, in *Proceedings of the International Colloquium on Computing, Communication, Control and Management* (IEEE Press, 2008), pp. 79–83
10. K.S. Cheung, K.O. Chow, Compositional synthesis of augmented marked graphs for manufacturing system integration, in *Proceedings of the IEEE International Conference on Integration Technology* (IEEE Press, 2007), pp. 287–292

Chapter 8
Manufacturing System Integration

This chapter illustrates the practical application of augmented marked graphs in manufacturing system design and integration. It starts with introducing manufacturing system design where the challenges in system integration are highlighted. We show how augmented marked graphs can be used for modelling the components of a typical manufacturing system. Then, we show how these augmented marked graphs can be composed as an integrated manufacturing system whose properties can be effectively analyzed.

8.1 Manufacturing System Design

A manufacturing system is basically an event-driven system that exhibits some concurrent, sequential, competitive and coordinated processes among its components or modules. These processes are mostly asynchronous in nature and often compete with each other for common resources. In manufacturing system design, a component-based approach is adopted, where a system is synthesized from its components or modules [1–5]. A key concern is to ensure the design correctness of the integrated system.

In the literature, Petri-net-based synthesis methods are proposed for manufacturing system design. Petri-nets are adopted because of their formal representation of concurrency and rigorous analysis of the system properties [6–13]. The applications of augmented marked graphs for manufacturing system design are well-founded. Cheung proposed the use of augmented marked graphs in modelling and analyzing manufacturing systems [14–17]. The synthesis of manufacturing system was studied, based on the property-preserving composition of augmented marked graphs [17–20].

In manufacturing system design, due to the interaction, inter-relation or inter-dependence among different components or modules, there exist concurrent and asynchronous processes, competing for some common resources, where erroneous situations such as deadlock and capacity overflow would be incurred. A number of issues and concerns arising from the concurrency and sharing of common resources

K.S. Cheung, *Augmented Marked Graphs*, DOI 10.1007/978-3-319-06428-4_8,
© Springer International Publishing Switzerland 2014

have to be resolved in order to obtain an integrated system which is free from erroneous situations. These are difficult challenges that a system designer has to face in manufacturing system integration. In the following, we highlight and elaborate these challenges.

Typically, the resources of a manufacturing system are scarce and used to be maximally shared among different components. For this reason, multiple components would compete for the same resources. This may however lead to deadlock if the system is not carefully designed and analyzed. Hence, deadlock freedom and liveness are considered as important properties of the integrated system. In the realm of manufacturing system engineering, avoidance of deadlock is a challenge in system design and integration.

In a manufacturing system, the components never have unlimited capacities. For example, a material storage buffer has a designated limit; an assembly job queue may accommodate up to a certain number of jobs. In manufacturing system design, the system designer must be aware that the capacity of each component cannot exceed its defined limit anytime. Hence, the absence of capacity overflow is also considered as an important property in the integrated system. Avoidance of capacity overflow is an objective in system design.

Another desirable property for any automated systems, including manufacturing systems, is that the system can be reinitialized from any reachable state. This property is sometimes called reversibility or recoverability, and is also a concern in manufacturing system design. Reversibility, together with liveness (implying freeness from deadlock) and boundedness (implying freeness of capacity overflow) are the desirable properties of an integrated manufacturing system. Hence, a key objective in manufacturing system integration is to ensure these desirable properties of the integrated system.

As mentioned in the previous chapter, to tackle the challenges in system integration, formal and mathematically sound techniques are essentially required in modelling the components and analyzing the properties of the integrated system. In this chapter, we show how augmented marked graphs or proper augmented marked graphs can be effectively used for modelling the components of a manufacturing system. Based on the properties of augmented marked graphs, the system designer can effectively check the desirable properties of the components, such as liveness, boundedness, reversibility and conservativeness. Then, it follows from the property-preserving composition of augmented marked graphs, the liveness, boundedness, reversibility and conservativeness of the integrated system can be effectively derived and analyzed.

8.2 Modelling and Analysis Using Augmented Marked Graphs

A manufacturing system is considered as a component-based system, so the modelling, integration and analysis process basically follows the steps in component-based system design.

Step 1. Modelling the components as proper augmented marked graphs.

Suppose that a set of manufacturing system components $C_1, C_2, \ldots, C_n$ are identified. For each C_i, specify the behavioural pattern of C_i as a proper augmented marked graph $(N_i, M_{i0}; R_i)$, where R_i represents the common resources to be used by C_i.

Step 2. Composing the components as an integrated system.

Obtained an integrated augmented marked graph $(N, M_0; R)$ by composing $(N_1, M_{10}; R_1), (N_2, M_{20}; R_2), \ldots, (N_n, M_{n0}; R_n)$ via their common resource places.

Step 3. Analyzing the properties of the individual components.

Based on the theories in Chaps. 3 and 4, check the liveness, boundedness, reversibility and conservativeness of each component represented by $(N_i, M_{i0}; R_i)$.

Step 4. Analyzing the properties of the integrated system.

Based on the theories in Chap. 5, check the liveness, boundedness, reversibility and conservativeness of the integrated manufacturing system represented by $(N, M_0; R)$.

It would then be concluded whether the integrated manufacturing system is live, bounded, reversibile and conservative.

8.3 Examples for Illustration

In the following, we illustrate the modelling, integration and analysis of manufacturing systems using augmented marked graphs. Four simple manufacturing systems are presented for illustration.

Example 8.1 It is a simple flexible workstation system for the production of circuit boards, extracted from [13] (pp. 121–124). The system consists of two robots M_1 and M_2, one feeder and one PCB area, as shown in Fig. 8.1. The system is structured as two components, C_1 and C_2. C_1 is responsible for the production of circuit boards by M_1 while C_2 is for the production of circuit boards by M_2.

Component C_1   The production process involves M_1, the feeder and the PCB area. Once the feeder is available, M_1 picks the required materials from the feeder and requests the PCB area. Once the PCB area is available, the feeder is released and the materials are moved into the PCB area for assembly. After assembly, the finished circuit board is moved out and the PCB area is released.

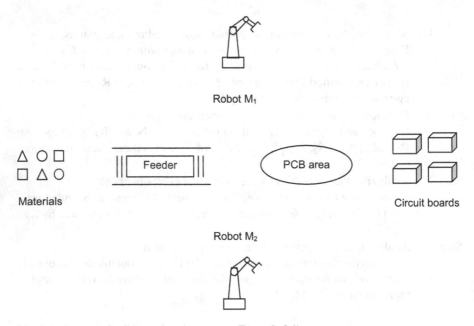

Fig. 8.1   A simple flexible workstation system (Example 8.1)

Component C_2   The production process involves M_2, the feeder and the PCB area. Once the feeder is available, M_2 picks the required materials from the feeder and requests the PCB area. Once the PCB area is available, the feeder is released and the materials are moved into the PCB area for assembly. After assembly, the finished circuit board is moved out and the PCB area is released.

Component C_1 is specified as augmented marked graph $(N_1, M_{10}; R_1)$, where $R_1 = \{r_{11}, r_{12}\}$. C_2 is specified as $(N_2, M_{20}; R_2)$, where $R_2 = \{r_{21}, r_{22}\}$. They are shown in Fig. 8.2 while Tables 8.1 and 8.2 state the semantic meanings of places and transitions, respectively.

For $(N_1, M_{10}; R_1)$ and $(N_2, M_{20}; R_2)$, $r_{11} \in R_1$ and $r_{21} \in R_2$ refer to the feeder area, and $r_{12} \in R_1$ and $r_{22} \in R_2$ refer to the PCB area. The feeder area and the PCB area are the common resources which are shared and competed between C_1 and C_2. $(N_1, M_{10}; R_1)$ and $(N_2, M_{20}; R_2)$ are to be composed via these common resource places. Figure 8.3 shows the integrated augmented marked graph $(N, M_0; R)$ obtained by composing $(N_1, M_{10}; R_1)$ and $(N_2, M_{20}; R_2)$ via $\{(r_{11}, r_{21}), (r_{12}, r_{22})\}$, while Tables 8.3 and 8.4 state the semantic meanings of places and transitions, respectively. For $(N, M_0; R)$ where $R = R_F = \{r_1, r_2\}$, r_1 is the place obtained by fusing r_{11} and r_{21}, and r_2 is the place obtained by fusing r_{12} and r_{22}.

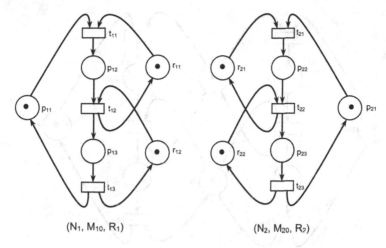

Fig. 8.2 Modelling of components as augmented marked graphs $(N_1, M_{10}; R_1)$ and $(N_2, M_{20}; R_2)$

Table 8.1 Semantic meanings of the places in the augmented marked graphs shown in Fig. 8.2

Place	Semantic meaning
p_{11}	M_1 is ready
p_{12}	M_1 is picking materials from the feeder
p_{13}	M_1 is assembling materials in the PCB area
p_{21}	M_2 is ready
p_{22}	M_2 is picking materials from the feeder
p_{23}	M_2 is assembling materials in the PCB area
r_{11}	The feeder is available
r_{12}	The PCB area is available
r_{21}	The feeder is available
r_{22}	The PCB area is available

Table 8.2 Semantic meanings of the transitions in the augmented marked graphs shown in Fig. 8.2

Transition	Semantic meaning
t_{11}	B_1 starts picking materials
t_{12}	B_1 finishes picking materials and starts assembling
t_{13}	B_1 finishes assembling and moves out the finished circuit board
t_{21}	B_2 starts picking materials
t_{22}	B_2 finishes picking materials and starts assembling
t_{23}	B_2 finishes assembling and moves out the finished circuit board

Let us analyze the properties of components C_1 and C_2. Consider $(N_1, M_{10}; R_1)$. Every place in R_1 satisfies the cycle-inclusion property. The siphon-trap property is satisfied, and every siphon would never become empty. According to Properties 3.11 and 3.12, $(N_1, M_{10}; R_1)$ is live and reversible. Similarly, $(N_2, M_{20}; R_2)$ is live and reversible. Besides, $(N_1, M_{10}; R_1)$ and $(N_2, M_{20}; R_2)$ are proper augmented marked graphs. According to Property 4.3, they are bounded and conservative. Hence, both C_1 and C_2 are live, bounded, reversible and conservative.

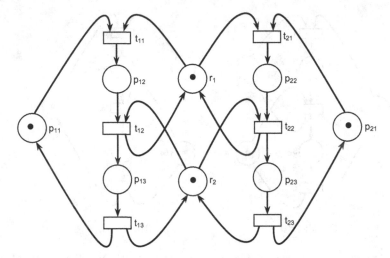

Fig. 8.3 The integrated augmented marked graphs $(N, M_0; R)$ obtained by composing $(N_1, M_{10}; R_1)$ and $(N_2, M_{20}; R_2)$ in Fig. 8.2

Table 8.3 Semantic meanings of the places in the augmented marked graph shown in Fig. 8.3

Place	Semantic meaning
p_{11}	M_1 is ready
p_{12}	M_1 is picking materials from the feeder
p_{13}	M_1 is assembling materials in the PCB area
p_{21}	M_2 is ready
p_{22}	M_2 is picking materials from the feeder
p_{23}	M_2 is assembling materials in the PCB area
r_1	The feeder is available
r_2	The PCB area is available

Table 8.4 Semantic meanings of the transitions in the augmented marked graph shown in Fig. 8.3

Transition	Semantic meaning
t_{11}	B_1 starts picking materials
t_{12}	B_1 finishes picking materials and starts assembling
t_{13}	B_1 finishes assembling and moves out the finished circuit board
t_{21}	B_2 starts picking materials
t_{22}	B_2 finishes picking materials and starts assembling
t_{23}	B_2 finishes assembling and moves out the finished circuit board

Consider the integrated augmented marked graph $(N, M_0; R)$. Since $(N_1, M_{10}; R_1)$ and $(N_2, M_{20}; R_2)$ are bounded and conservative, according to Properties 5.7 and 5.8, $(N, M_0; R)$ is bounded and conservative. For $(N, M_0; R)$ where $R_F = \{r_1, r_2\}$, both r_1 and r_2 satisfy the cycle-inclusion property, and hence every R_F-siphon would never become empty. According to Properties 5.4 and 5.5, $(N, M_0; R)$ is live and reversible. Hence, it may be concluded that the integrated system is live, bounded, reversible and conservative.

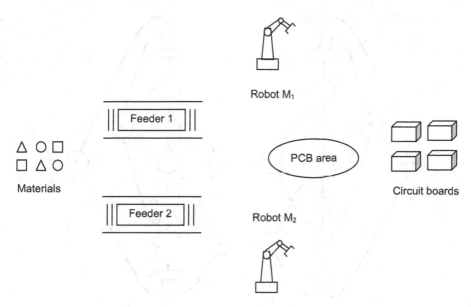

Fig. 8.4 A simple flexible workstation system (Example 8.2)

Example 8.2 It is a revised version of Example 8.1, where one more feeder is added. In this revised version, the simple flexible workstation system consists of two robots M_1 and M_2, two feeders F_1 and F_2, and one PCB area, as shown in Fig. 8.4. The system is structured as two components, C_1 and C_2. C_1 is responsible for the production of circuit boards by M_1 while C_2 is for the production of circuit boards by M_2.

Component C_1 The production process involves M_1, F_1 and F_2, and the PCB area. Once F_1 is available, M_1 picks the required materials from F_1 and requests F_2. Once F_2 is available, M_1 picks the required materials from F_2 and requests the PCB area. Once the PCB area is available, F_1 and F_2 are released and the materials are moved into the PCB area for assembly. After assembly, the finished circuit board is moved out and the PCB area is released.

Component C_2 The production process involves M_2, F_1 and F_2, and the PCB area. Once F_2 is available, M_2 picks the required materials from F_2 and requests F_1. Once F_1 is available, M_2 picks the required materials from F_1 and requests the PCB area. Once the PCB area is available, F_1 and F_2 are released and the materials are moved into the PCB area for assembly. After assembly, the finished circuit board is moved out and the PCB area is released.

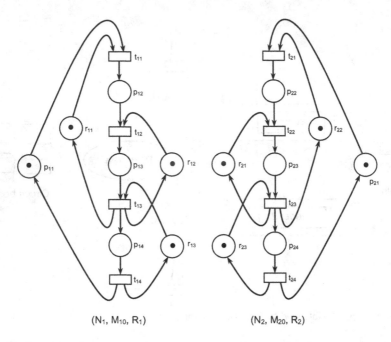

(N₁, M₁₀, R₁)   (N₂, M₂₀, R₂)

Fig. 8.5 Modelling of components as augmented marked graphs $(N_1, M_{10}; R_1)$ and $(N_2, M_{20}; R_2)$

Place	Semantic meaning
Table 8.5 Semantic meanings of the places in the augmented marked graphs shown in Fig. 8.5	
p_{11}	M_1 is ready
p_{12}	M_1 is picking materials from F_1
p_{13}	M_1 is picking materials from F_1 and F_2
p_{14}	M_1 is assembling materials in the PCB area
p_{21}	M_2 is ready
p_{22}	M_2 is picking materials from F_2
p_{23}	M_2 is picking materials from F_1 and F_2
p_{24}	M_2 is assembling materials in the PCB area
r_{11}	F_1 is available
r_{12}	F_2 is available
r_{13}	The PCB area is available
r_{21}	F_1 is available
r_{22}	F_2 is available
r_{23}	The PCB area is available

Component C_1 is specified as augmented marked graph $(N_1, M_{10}; R_1)$, where $R_1 = \{r_{11}, r_{12}, r_{13}\}$. C_2 is specified as $(N_2, M_{20}; R_2)$, where $R_2 = \{r_{21}, r_{22}, r_{23}\}$. They are shown in Fig. 8.5 while Tables 8.5 and 8.6 state the semantic meanings of places and transitions, respectively.

For $(N_1, M_{10}; R_1)$ and $(N_2, M_{20}; R_2)$, $r_{11} \in R_1$ and $r_{21} \in R_2$ refer to F_1, $r_{12} \in R_1$ and $r_{22} \in R_2$ refer to F_2, and $r_{13} \in R_1$ and $r_{23} \in R_2$ refer to the PCB area. The feeders F_1 and F_2 and the PCB area are the common resources which are shared and competed between C_1 and C_2. $(N_1, M_{10}; R_1)$ and $(N_2, M_{20}; R_2)$ are to be composed

Table 8.6 Semantic meanings of the transitions in the augmented marked graphs shown in Fig. 8.5

Transition	Semantic meaning
t_{11}	B_1 starts picking materials from F_1
t_{12}	B_1 starts picking materials from F_2
t_{13}	B_1 finishes picking materials and starts assembling
t_{14}	B_1 finishes assembling and moves out the finished circuit board
t_{21}	B_2 starts picking materials from F_2
t_{22}	B_2 starts picking materials from F_1
t_{23}	B_2 finishes picking materials and starts assembling
t_{24}	B_2 finishes assembling and moves out the finished circuit board

via these common resource places. Figure 8.6 shows the integrated augmented marked graph $(N, M_0; R)$ obtained by composing $(N_1, M_{10}; R_1)$ and $(N_2, M_{20}; R_2)$ via $\{(r_{11}, r_{21}), (r_{12}, r_{22}), (r_{13}, r_{23})\}$, while Tables 8.7 and 8.8 state the semantic meanings of places and transitions, respectively.

For $(N, M_0; R)$ where $R = R_F = \{r_1, r_2, r_3\}$, r_1 is the place obtained by fusing r_{11} and r_{21}, r_2 is the place obtained by fusing r_{12} and r_{22}, and r_3 is the place obtained by fusing r_{13} and r_{23}.

Let us analyze the properties of components C_1 and C_2. Consider $(N_1, M_{10}; R_1)$. Every place in R_1 satisfies the cycle-inclusion property. The siphon-trap property is satisfied, and every siphon would never become empty. According to Properties 3.11 and 3.12, $(N_1, M_{10}; R_1)$ is live and reversible. Similarly, $(N_2, M_{20}; R_2)$ is live and reversible. Besides, $(N_1, M_{10}; R_1)$ and $(N_2, M_{20}; R_2)$ are proper augmented marked graphs. According to Property 4.3, they are bounded and conservative. Hence, both C_1 and C_2 are live, bounded, reversible and conservative.

Consider the integrated augmented marked graph $(N, M_0; R)$. Since $(N_1, M_{10}; R_1)$ and $(N_2, M_{20}; R_2)$ are bounded and conservative, according to Properties 5.7 and 5.8, $(N, M_0; R)$ is bounded and conservative. For $(N, M_0; R)$ where $R_F = \{r_1, r_2, r_3\}$, $S = \langle p_{13}, p_{23}, r_1, r_2 \rangle$ is a R_F-siphon which would become empty on firing the transitions $\langle t_{11}, t_{21} \rangle$. According to Property 5.4, $(N, M_0; R)$ is neither live nor reversible. Hence, it may be concluded that the integrated system is bounded and conservative, but neither live nor reversible.

Example 8.3 It is a simple flexible assembly system for assembling materials from conveyors, extracted from [8] (pp. 58–61). The system consists of three robots M_1, M_2 and M_3, and three conveyors Y_1, Y_2 and Y_3, as shown in Fig. 8.7. The system is structured as three components, C_1, C_2 and C_3. C_1 is responsible for the assembly of materials in Y_1, C_2 is for the assembly of materials in Y_2, and C_3 is for the assembly of materials in Y_3.

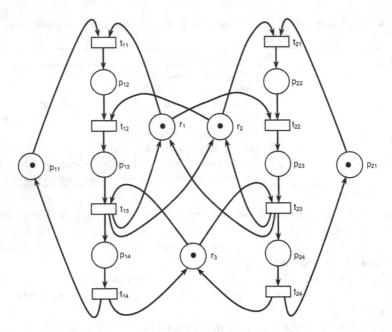

Fig. 8.6 The integrated augmented marked graphs $(N, M_0; R)$ obtained by composing $(N_1, M_{10}; R_1)$ and $(N_2, M_{20}; R_2)$ in Fig. 8.5

Table 8.7 Semantic meanings of the places in the augmented marked graph shown in Fig. 8.6

Place	Semantic meaning
p_{11}	M_1 is ready
p_{12}	M_1 is picking materials from F_1
p_{13}	M_1 is picking materials from F_1 and F_2
p_{14}	M_1 is assembling materials in the PCB area
p_{21}	M_2 is ready
p_{22}	M_2 is picking materials from F_2
p_{23}	M_2 is picking materials from F_1 and F_2
p_{24}	M_2 is assembling materials in the PCB area
r_1	F_1 is available
r_2	F_2 is available
r_3	The PCB area is available

Component C_1   The assembly process involves Y_1, M_1 and M_2. On receipt of materials in Y_1 and when M_1 is available, M_1 is acquired. M_2 is then requested. When M_2 is available, M_2 is acquired. After acquired both M_1 and M_2, assembly of materials begins. Both M_1 and M_2 are released after the assembly.

Component C_2   The assembly process involves Y_2, M_2 and M_3. On receipt of materials in Y_2, and when M_2 is available, M_2 is acquired. M_3 is then requested. When M_3 is available, M_3 is acquired. After

Table 8.8 Semantic meanings of the transitions in the augmented marked graph shown in Fig. 8.6

Transition	Semantic meaning
t_{11}	B_1 starts picking materials from F_1
t_{12}	B_1 starts picking materials from F_2
t_{13}	B_1 finishes picking materials and starts assembling
t_{14}	B_1 finishes assembling and moves out the finished circuit board
t_{21}	B_2 starts picking materials from F_2
t_{22}	B_2 starts picking materials from F_1
t_{23}	B_2 finishes picking materials and starts assembling
t_{24}	B_2 finishes assembling and moves out the finished circuit board

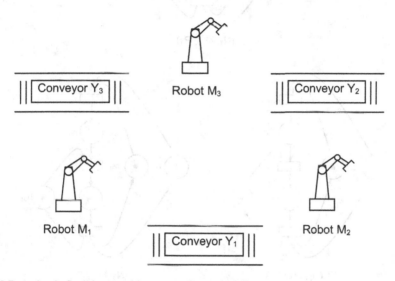

Fig. 8.7 A simple flexible assembly system (Example 8.3)

acquired both M_2 and M_3, assembly of materials begins. Both M_2 and M_3 are released after the assembly.

Component C_3 The assembly process involves Y_3, M_1 and M_3. On receipt of materials in Y_3, and when M_3 is available, M_3 is acquired. M_1 is then requested. When M_1 is available, M_1 is acquired. After acquiring both M_1 and M_3, assembly of materials begins. Both M_1 and M_3 are released after the assembly.

Component C_1 is specified as augmented marked graph $(N_1, M_{10}; R_1)$, where $R_1 = \{r_{11}, r_{12}\}$. Component C_2 is specified as $(N_2, M_{20}; R_2)$, where $R_2 = \{r_{22}, r_{23}\}$. Component C_3 is specified as $(N_3, M_{30}; R_3)$, where $R_3 = \{r_{33}, r_{31}\}$. They are shown in Fig. 8.8 while Tables 8.9 and 8.10 state the semantic meanings of places and transitions, respectively.

For $(N_1, M_{10}; R_1)$, $(N_2, M_{20}; R_2)$ and $(N_3, M_{30}; R_3)$, $r_{11} \in R_1$ and $r_{31} \in R_3$ refer to M_1, $r_{12} \in R_1$ and $r_{22} \in R_2$ refer to M_2, and $r_{23} \in R_2$ and $r_{33} \in R_3$ refer to M_3.

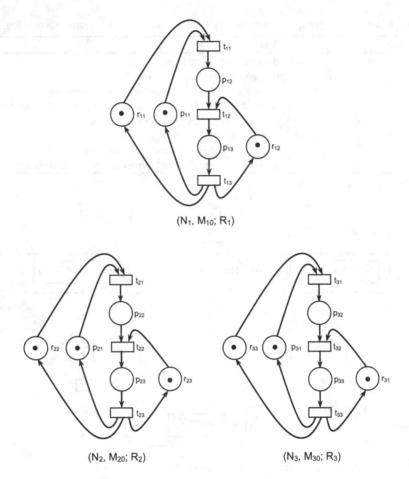

$(N_1, M_{10}; R_1)$

$(N_2, M_{20}; R_2)$ $(N_3, M_{30}; R_3)$

Fig. 8.8 Modelling of components as augmented marked graphs $(N_1, M_{10}; R_1)$, $(N_2, M_{20}; R_2)$ and $(N_3, M_{30}; R_3)$

Robots M_1, M_2 and M_3 are the common resources which are shared and competed among C_1, C_2 and C_3. $(N_1, M_{10}; R_1)$, $(N_2, M_{20}; R_2)$ and $(N_3, M_{30}; R_3)$ are to be composed via their common resource places. Figure 8.9 shows the integrated augmented marked graph $(N', M_0'; R')$ obtained by composing $(N_1, M_{10}; R_1)$ and $(N_2, M_{20}; R_2)$ via $\{(r_{12}, r_{22})\}$. For $(N', M_0'; R')$ where $R' = \{r_{11}, r_2, r_{23}\}$, r_2 is the place obtained by fusing r_{12} and r_{22}.

Figure 8.10 shows the final integrated augmented marked graph $(N, M_0; R)$ obtained by composing $(N', M_0'; R')$ and $(N_3, M_{30}; R_3)$ via $\{(r_{11}, r_{31}), (r_{23}, r_{33})\}$, while Tables 8.11 and 8.12 state the semantic meanings of places and transitions, respectively. For $(N, M_0; R)$ where $R = R_F = \{r_1, r_2, r_3\}$, r_1 is the place obtained by fusing r_{11} and r_{31}, and r_3 is the place obtained by fusing r_{23} and r_{33}.

Table 8.9 Semantic meanings of the places in the augmented marked graphs shown in Fig. 8.8

Place	Semantic meaning
p_{11}	Y_1 is ready
p_{12}	Y_1 is occupying M_1
p_{13}	Y_1 is occupying M_1 and M_2 to perform assembly
p_{21}	Y_2 is ready
p_{22}	Y_2 is occupying M_2
p_{23}	Y_2 is occupying M_2 and M_3 to perform assembly
p_{31}	Y_3 is ready
p_{32}	Y_3 is occupying M_3
p_{33}	Y_3 is occupying M_1 and M_3 to perform assembly
r_{11}	R_1 is available
r_{12}	R_2 is available
r_{22}	R_2 is available
r_{23}	R_3 is available
r_{31}	R_1 is available
r_{33}	R_3 is available

Table 8.10 Semantic meanings of the transitions in the augmented marked graphs shown in Fig. 8.8

Transition	Semantic meaning
t_{11}	Y_1 acquires M_1
t_{12}	Y_1 acquires M_2
t_{13}	Y_1 releases M_1 and M_2
t_{21}	Y_2 acquires M_2
t_{22}	Y_2 acquires M_3
t_{23}	Y_2 releases M_2 and M_3
t_{31}	Y_3 acquires M_3
t_{32}	Y_3 acquires M_1
t_{33}	Y_3 releases M_1 and M_3

Let us analyze the properties of components C_1, C_2 and C_3. Consider $(N_1, M_{10}; R_1)$. Every place in R_1 satisfies the cycle-inclusion property. The siphon-trap property is satisfied, and every siphon would never become empty. According to Properties 3.11 and 3.12, $(N_1, M_{10}; R_1)$ is live and reversible. Similarly, $(N_2, M_{20}; R_2)$ and $(N_3, M_{30}; R_3)$ are live and reversible. Besides, $(N_1, M_{10}; R_1)$, $(N_2, M_{20}; R_2)$ and $(N_3, M_{30}; R_3)$ are proper augmented marked graphs. According to Property 4.3, they are bounded and conservative. Hence, C_1, C_2 and C_3 are live, bounded, reversible and conservative.

Consider the integrated augmented marked graph $(N', M_0'; R')$. Since both $(N_1, M_{10}; R_1)$ and $(N_2, M_{20}; R_2)$ are bounded and conservative, according to Properties 5.7 and 5.8, $(N', M_0'; R')$ is bounded and conservative. For $(N', M_0'; R')$ where $R_F' = \{r_2\}$, r_2 satisfies the cycle-inclusion property, and hence, every R_F-siphon would never become empty. According to Properties 5.4 and 5.5, $(N', M_0'; R')$ is live and reversible.

Next, consider the final integrated augmented marked graph $(N, M_0; R)$. Since both $(N', M_0'; R')$ and $(N_3, M_{30}; R_3)$ are bounded and conservative, according to

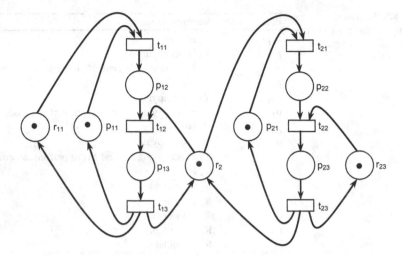

Fig. 8.9 The integrated augmented marked graph $(N', M_0'; R')$ obtained by composing $(N_1, M_{10}; R_1)$ and $(N_2, M_{20}; R_2)$ in Fig. 8.8

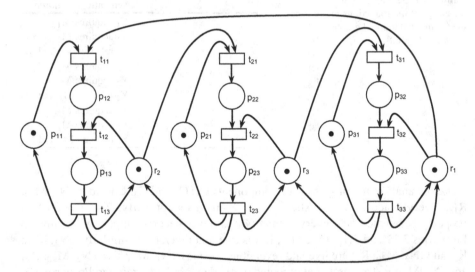

Fig. 8.10 The final integrated augmented marked graph $(N, M_0; R)$ obtained by composing $(N_3, M_{30}; R_3)$ and $(N', M_0'; R')$ in Figs. 8.8 and 8.9

Properties 5.7 and 5.8, $(N, M_0; R)$ is bounded and conservative. For $(N, M_0; R)$ where $R_F = \{r_1, r_3\}$, $S = \langle r_1, r_2, r_3, p_{13}, p_{23}, p_{33} \rangle$ is a R_F-siphon which would become empty on firing the transitions $\langle t_{12}, t_{22}, t_{32} \rangle$. According to Property 5.4, $(N, M_0; R)$ is neither live nor reversible. Hence, it may be concluded that the integrated system is bounded and conservative, but neither live nor reversible. It is not well-behaved.

Table 8.11 Semantic meanings of the places in the augmented marked graph shown in Fig. 8.10

Place	Semantic meaning
p_{11}	Y_1 is ready
p_{12}	Y_1 is occupying M_1
p_{13}	Y_1 is occupying M_1 and M_2 to perform assembly
p_{21}	Y_2 is ready
p_{22}	Y_2 is occupying M_2
p_{23}	Y_2 is occupying M_2 and M_3 to perform assembly
p_{31}	Y_3 is ready
p_{32}	Y_3 is occupying M_3
p_{33}	Y_3 is occupying M_1 and M_3 to perform assembly
r_1	R_1 is available
r_2	R_2 is available
r_3	R_3 is available

Table 8.12 Semantic meanings of the transitions in the augmented marked graph shown in Fig. 8.10

Transition	Semantic meaning
t_{11}	Y_1 acquires M_1
t_{12}	Y_1 acquires M_2
t_{13}	Y_1 releases M_1 and M_2
t_{21}	Y_2 acquires M_2
t_{22}	Y_2 acquires M_3
t_{23}	Y_2 releases M_2 and M_3
t_{31}	Y_3 acquires M_3
t_{32}	Y_3 acquires M_1
t_{33}	Y_3 releases M_1 and M_3

Example 8.4 It is a revised version of Example 8.3, where one more robot M_4 is added. In this revised version, the simple flexible assembly system consists of four robots M_1, M_2, M_3 and M_4 and three conveyors Y_1, Y_2 and Y_3, as shown in Fig. 8.11. The system is structured as three components, C_1, C_2 and C_3. C_1 is responsible for the assembly of materials in Y_1, C_2 is for the assembly of materials in Y_2, and C_3 is for the assembly of materials in Y_3.

Component C_1 The assembly process involves Y_1, M_1, M_2 and M_4. On receipt of materials in Y_1, and when both M_1 and M_4 are available, M_1 and M_4 are acquired. M_2 is then requested. When M_2 is available, M_2 is acquired and M_4 is released. Assembly of materials then begins. Both M_1 and M_2 are released after the assembly.

Component C_2 The assembly process involves Y_2, M_2, M_3 and M_4. On receipt of materials in Y_2, and when both M_2 and M_4 are available, M_2 and M_4 are acquired. M_3 is then requested. When M_3 is available, M_3 is acquired and M_4 is released. Assembly of materials then begins. Both M_2 and M_3 are released after the assembly.

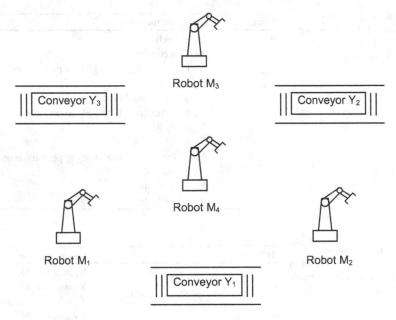

Fig. 8.11 A revised flexible assembly system (Example 8.4)

Component C₃   The assembly process involves Y_3, M_1 and M_3. On receipt of materials in Y_3, and when M_3 is available, M_3 is acquired. M_1 is then requested. When M_1 is available, M_1 is acquired. After acquiring both M_1 and M_3, assembly of materials begins. Both M_1 and M_3 are released after the assembly.

Component C_1 is specified as augmented marked graph $(N_1, M_{10}; R_1)$, where $R_1 = \{r_{11}, r_{12}, r_{14}\}$. Component C_2 is specified as $(N_2, M_{20}; R_2)$, where $R_2 = \{r_{22}, r_{23}, r_{24}\}$. Component C_3 is specified as $(N_3, M_{30}; R_3)$, where $R_3 = \{r_{33}, r_{31}\}$. They are shown in Fig. 8.12 while Tables 8.13 and 8.14 state the semantic meanings of places and transitions, respectively.

For $(N_1, M_{10}; R_1)$, $(N_2, M_{20}; R_2)$ and $(N_3, M_{30}; R_3)$, $r_{11} \in R_1$ and $r_{31} \in R_3$ refer to M_1, $r_{12} \in R_1$ and $r_{22} \in R_2$ refer to M_2, $r_{23} \in R_2$ and $r_{33} \in R_3$ refer to M_3, and $r_{14} \in R_1$ and $r_{24} \in R_2$ refer to R_4. Robots M_1, M_2, M_3 and M_4 are the common resources which are shared and competed among C_1, C_2 and C_3. $(N_1, M_{10}; R_1)$, $(N_2, M_{20}; R_2)$ and $(N_3, M_{30}; R_3)$ are to be composed via their common resource places. Figure 8.13 shows the integrated augmented marked graph $(N', M_0'; R')$ obtained by composing $(N_1, M_{10}; R_1)$ and $(N_2, M_{20}; R_2)$ via $\{(r_{12}, r_{22}), (r_{14}, r_{24})\}$. For $(N', M_0'; R')$ where $R' = \{r_{11}, r_2, r_{23}, r_4\}$, r_2 is the place obtained by fusing r_{12} and r_{22}, and r_4 is the place obtained by fusing r_{14} and r_{24}.

Figure 8.14 shows the final integrated augmented marked graph $(N, M_0; R)$ obtained by composing $(N', M_0'; R')$ and $(N_3, M_{30}; R_3)$ via $\{(r_{11}, r_{31}), (r_{23}, r_{33})\}$,

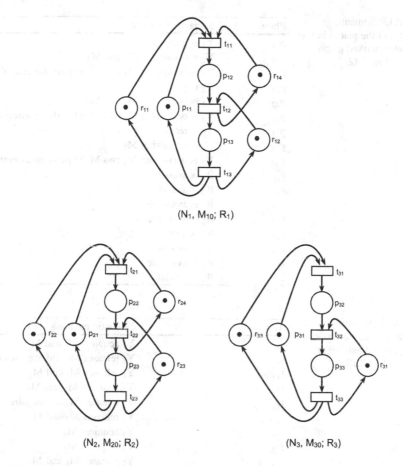

$(N_1, M_{10}; R_1)$

$(N_2, M_{20}; R_2)$ $(N_3, M_{30}; R_3)$

Fig. 8.12 Modelling of components as augmented marked graphs $(N_1, M_{10}; R_1)$, $(N_2, M_{20}; R_2)$ and $(N_3, M_{30}; R_3)$

while Tables 8.15 and 8.16 state the semantic meanings of places and transitions, respectively. For $(N, M_0; R)$ where $R = \{r_1, r_2, r_3\}$, r_1 is the place obtained by fusing r_{11} and r_{31}, and r_3 is the place obtained by fusing r_{23} and r_{33}.

Let us analyze the properties of components C_1, C_2 and C_3. Consider $(N_1, M_{10}; R_1)$. Every place in R_1 satisfies the cycle-inclusion property. The siphon-trap property is satisfied, and every siphon would never become empty. According to Properties 3.11 and 3.12, $(N_1, M_{10}; R_1)$ is live and reversible. Similarly, $(N_2, M_{20}; R_2)$ and $(N_3, M_{30}; R_3)$ are live and reversible. Besides, $(N_1, M_{10}; R_1)$, $(N_2, M_{20}; R_2)$ and $(N_3, M_{30}; R_3)$ are proper augmented marked graphs. According to Property 4.3, they are bounded and conservative.

Consider the integrated augmented marked graph $(N', M_0'; R')$. Since both $(N_1, M_{10}; R_1)$ and $(N_2, M_{20}; R_2)$ are bounded and conservative, according to Properties

Table 8.13 Semantic meanings of the places in the augmented marked graphs shown in Fig. 8.12

Place	Semantic meaning
p_{11}	Y_1 is ready
p_{12}	Y_1 is occupying M_1 and M_4
p_{13}	Y_1 is occupying M_1 and M_2 to perform assembly
p_{21}	Y_2 is ready
p_{22}	Y_2 is occupying M_2 and M_4
p_{23}	Y_2 is occupying M_2 and M_3 to perform assembly
p_{31}	Y_3 is ready
p_{32}	Y_3 is occupying M_3
p_{33}	Y_3 is occupying M_1 and M_3 to perform assembly
r_{11}	R_1 is available
r_{12}	R_2 is available
r_{14}	R_4 is available
r_{22}	R_2 is available
r_{23}	R_3 is available
r_{24}	R_4 is available
r_{31}	R_1 is available
r_{33}	R_3 is available

Table 8.14 Semantic meanings of the transitions in the augmented marked graphs shown in Fig. 8.12

Transition	Semantic meaning
t_{11}	Y_1 acquires M_1 and M_4
t_{12}	Y_1 releases M_4 and acquires M_2
t_{13}	Y_1 releases M_1 and M_2
t_{21}	Y_2 acquires M_2 and M_4
t_{22}	Y_2 releases M_4 and acquires M_3
t_{23}	Y_2 releases M_2 and M_3
t_{31}	Y_3 acquires M_3
t_{32}	Y_3 acquires M_1
t_{33}	Y_3 releases M_1 and M_3

5.7 and 5.8, $(N', M_0'; R')$ is bounded and conservative. For $(N', M_0'; R')$ where $R_F' = \{r_2\}$, r_2 satisfies the cycle-inclusion property, and hence every R_F-siphon would never become empty. According to Properties 5.4 and 5.5, $(N', M_0'; R')$ is live and reversible.

Next, consider the final integrated augmented marked graph $(N, M_0; R)$. Since both $(N', M_0'; R')$ and $(N_3, M_{30}; R_3)$ are bounded and conservative, according to Properties 5.7 and 5.8, $(N, M_0; R)$ is bounded and conservative. For $(N, M_0; R)$ where $R_F = \{r_1, r_3\}$, both r_1 and r_3 satisfy the cycle-inclusion property, and hence every R_F-siphon would never become empty. According to Properties 5.4 and 5.5, $(N, M_0; R)$ is live and reversible. Hence, it may be concluded that the integrated system is live, bounded, reversible and conservative.

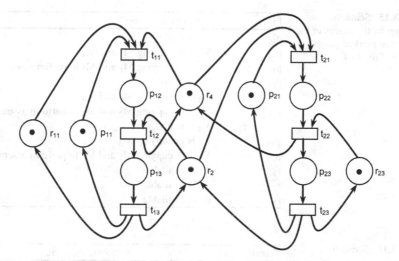

Fig. 8.13 The integrated augmented marked graph $(N', M_0'; R')$ obtained by composing $(N_1, M_{10}; R_1)$ and $(N_2, M_{20}; R_2)$ in Fig. 8.12

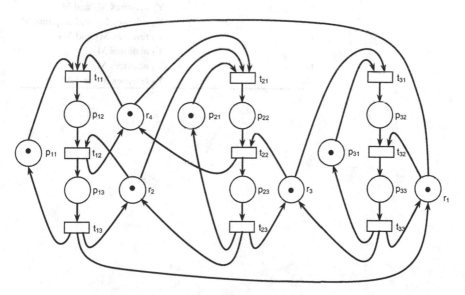

Fig. 8.14 The final integrated augmented marked graph $(N, M_0; R)$ obtained by composing $(N_3, M_{30}; R_3)$ and $(N', M_0'; R')$ in Figs. 8.12 and 8.13

Table 8.15 Semantic meanings of the places in the augmented marked graph shown in Fig. 8.14

Place	Semantic meaning
p_{11}	Y_1 is ready
p_{12}	Y_1 is occupying M_1 and M_4
p_{13}	Y_1 is occupying M_1 and M_2 to perform assembly
p_{21}	Y_2 is ready
p_{22}	Y_2 is occupying M_2 and M_4
p_{23}	Y_2 is occupying M_2 and M_3 to perform assembly
p_{31}	Y_3 is ready
p_{32}	Y_3 is occupying M_3
p_{33}	Y_3 is occupying M_1 and M_3 to perform assembly
r_1	R_1 is available
r_2	R_2 is available
r_3	R_3 is available

Table 8.16 Semantic meanings of the transitions in the augmented marked graph shown in Fig. 8.14

Transition	Semantic meaning
t_{11}	Y_1 acquires M_1 and M_4
t_{12}	Y_1 releases M_4 and acquires M_2
t_{13}	Y_1 releases M_1 and M_2
t_{21}	Y_2 acquires M_2 and M_4
t_{22}	Y_2 releases M_4 and acquires M_3
t_{23}	Y_2 releases M_2 and M_3
t_{31}	Y_3 acquires M_3
t_{32}	Y_3 acquires M_1
t_{33}	Y_3 releases M_1 and M_3

References

1. M.C. Zhou, K. McDermott, P.A. Patel, Petri net synthesis and analysis of a flexible manufacturing system cell. IEEE Trans. Syst. Man Cybern. **23**(2), 523–531 (1993)
2. M.D. Jeng, F. DiCesare, A review of synthesis techniques for petri nets with applications to automated manufacturing systems. IEEE Trans. Syst. Man Cybern. **23**(1), 301–312 (1993)
3. M.C. Zhou, F. DiCesare, *Petri Net Synthesis for Discrete Event Controls of Manufacturing Systems* (Kluwer Academic Publishers, Norwell, 1993)
4. M.D. Jeng, F. DiCesare, Synthesis using resource control nets for modeling shared-resource systems. IEEE Trans. Robot. Autom. **11**(3), 317–327 (1995)
5. M.D. Jeng, A petri net synthesis theory for modeling flexible manufacturing systems. IEEE Trans. Syst. Man Cybern. **27**(2), 169–183 (1997)
6. F. Dicesare et al., *Practice of Petri Nets in Manufacturing* (Chapman and Hall, London, 1993)
7. M. Silva, R. Valette, Petri nets and flexible manufacturing, in *Advances in Petri Nets 1989*, ed. by G. Rozenberg. Lecture Notes in Computer Science, vol. 424 (Springer, Berlin, 1989), pp. 374–417
8. A.A. Desrochers, R.Y. Al-Jaar, *Applications of Petri Nets in Manufacturing Systems* (IEEE Press, Piscataway, 1994)
9. M.C. Zhou, A.D. Robbi, Application of Petri methodology to manufacturing systems, in *Computer Control of Flexible Manufacturing Systems*, ed. by S.B. Joshi, J.S. Smith (Chapman and Hall, London, 1994), pp. 207–230
10. J.M. Proth, X. Xie, *Petri Nets: A Tool for Design and Management of Manufacturing Systems* (Wiley, Chichester, 1996)
11. K.E. Moore, S.M. Gupta, Petri Net models of flexible and automated manufacturing systems: a survey. Int. J. Prod. Res. **34**(11), 3001–3035 (1996)
12. M. Silva et al., Petri Nets and production systems, in *Lectures on Petri Nets II: Applications*, ed. by W. Reisig, G. Rozenberg. Lecture Notes in Computer Science, vol. 1492 (Springer, Berlin, 1998), pp. 85–124
13. M.C. Zhou, K. Venkatesh, *Modeling, Simulation and Control of Flexible Manufacturing Systems: A Petri Net Approach* (World Scientific, Singapore, 1999)
14. K.S. Cheung, K.O. Chow, Analysis of manufacturing systems based on augmented marked graphs, in *Proceedings of the International Conference on Computational Intelligence for Modelling, Control and Automation (CIMCA 2005)*, vol. 2 (IEEE Computer Society Press, 2005), pp. 847–851
15. K.S. Cheung, Modelling and analysis of manufacturing systems using augmented marked graphs. Inf. Technol. Control **35**(1), 19–26 (2006)
16. K.S. Cheung, K.O. Chow, Analysis of capacity overflow for manufacturing systems, in *Proceedings of the IEEE Conference on Automation Science and Engineering* (IEEE Press, 2006), pp. 331–335
17. K.S. Cheung, Augmented marked graphs and the analysis of shared resource systems, in *Petri Net: Theory and Application*, ed. by V. Kordic (ARS Publishing, 2007), pp. 377–400
18. K.S. Cheung, Composition of augmented marked graphs and its application to component-based system design. Inf. Technol. Control **36**(3), 310–317 (2007)
19. K.S. Cheung, K.O. Chow, Compositional synthesis of augmented marked graphs for manufacturing system integration, in *Proceedings of the IEEE International Conference on Integration Technology* (IEEE Press, 2007), pp. 287–292
20. K.S. Cheung, Composition of augmented marked graphs and its application to system integration, in *Proceedings of the International Colloquium on Computing, Communication, Control and Management* (IEEE Press, 2008), pp. 79–83

Chapter 9
Conclusion

This chapter briefly concludes this book. It summarizes the theories and application of augmented marked graphs, and discusses the possible direction of further studies.

9.1 Formal Techniques for Modelling and Analysis

Today's computer systems and automated systems are usually large and complex. Component-based system design is widely recognized as a promising approach to managing complexity and maximizing reuse of components or modules. In component-based system design, a system is designed and implemented in terms of components or modules. This inevitably enables the system designer to tackle the difficulties in designing large and complex systems by structuring a system into manageable components. This however creates another challenge—how to ensure the design correctness of the integrated system.

At the beginning of this book, we discuss the challenge in system integration, especially for systems involving concurrency and shared resources, where erroneous situations such as deadlock and capacity overflow would occur. It is also pointed out that the correctness of all components or modules does not guarantee that the integrated system is free from erroneous situations. To ensure the design correctness, the system designer needs to perform a painful exercise of walking through all possible execution scenarios of the system in order to identify any erroneous situation. Unarguably, formal or mathematically sound techniques for modelling and analysis would help resolve this challenge which has perplexed system designers of component-based systems for a long time. This book shows how augmented marked graphs can be effectively used for such purposes.

K.S. Cheung, *Augmented Marked Graphs*, DOI 10.1007/978-3-319-06428-4_9,
© Springer International Publishing Switzerland 2014

9.2   Theory and Application of Augmented Marked Graphs

We introduce augmented marked graphs by stating the formal definitions and known properties. Specifically, we present some siphon-based characterizations for live and reversible augmented marked graphs. A cycle-inclusion property introduced to provide an alternative means to characterize the siphon-trap property, and, hence, liveness and reversibility of augmented marked graphs. On the other hand, a R-transform is introduced for characterizing bounded and conservative augmented marked graphs. In accordance with these characterizations, algorithms for checking the liveness, boundedness, reversibility and conservativeness of augmented marked graphs are derived.

A special type of augmented marked graphs, proper augmented marked graphs slightly deviates from the original augmented marked graphs first defined in the literature. Proper augmented marked graphs are always bounded and conservative. The characterizations for live and reversible augmented marked graphs can also apply to proper augmented marked graphs.

We then investigate the composition of augmented marked graphs via common resource places. A special focus is placed on the preservation of properties, such as liveness, reversibility, boundedness and conservativeness. It is proved that boundedness and conservativeness are preserved in the composition. R_F-siphons are then defined for characterizing the liveness and reversibility of the integrated augmented marked graph. The composition of proper augmented marked graphs is also studied.

To illustrate the theories of augmented marked graphs, the dining philosophers problem is used for illustration. The problem is modelled as augmented marked graphs so that the liveness, boundedness, reversibility and conservativeness can be effectively analyzed through the characterizations for augmented marked graphs. The Dining Philosophers problem is also used for illustrating the composition of augmented marked graphs.

Following the theoretical description, we discuss the application of augmented marked graphs in system integration with an aim to address the challenges in ensuring design correctness of the integrated system. We show the conceptual application of augmented marked graphs in component-based system design, such as on the modelling of components, system integration, and analysis of the integrated system. We also show the practical application of augmented marked graphs in component-based system design, where some simple manufacturing systems are used for illustration. Given a set of manufacturing system components, we specify them as augmented marked graphs, perform system integration by the composition of these augmented marked graphs, and analyze the properties of the integrated system based on the theories of augmented marked graphs.

9.3 Possible Direction of Further Studies

This book provides a comprehensive description of augmented marked graphs. Further development in both the theoretical and application aspects is possible, as elaborated below.

In the theoretical aspect, the characterizations for live and reversible augmented marked graphs can be further explored. Basically, the siphon-trap property and cycle-inclusion property provide the sufficient conditions for live and reversible augmented marked graphs. In what circumstances would the siphon-trap property and cycle-inclusion property become not only a sufficient condition but also a necessary condition of deadlock freedom and thus liveness and reversibility for augmented marked graphs?

In the application aspect, we illustrate the conceptual application to system integration for component-based systems as well as the practical application to system integration for manufacturing systems. We may investigate other practical application areas, such as protocol engineering. As, for example, in communication protocol design, how can the composition of augmented marked graphs be effectively used for synthesizing an integrated protocol specification from a given set of communication scenarios?

Appendices: Summary of Theoretical Results

Appendix A: Properties of Augmented Marked Graphs

This appendix lists the properties of augmented marked graphs (Chap. 3) and proper augmented marked graphs (Chap. 4), and the properties pertaining to the composition of augmented marked graphs (Chap. 5).

Chapter 3: Augmented Marked Graphs

Property 3.1 Let $(N, M_0; R)$ be an augmented marked graph. For a minimal siphon S in $(N, M_0; R)$, there exists a set of cycles $Y \subseteq \Omega_N$ such that $P[Y] = S$.

Property 3.2 Let S be a minimal siphon of an augmented marked graph $(N, M_0; R)$. For every place $p \in S$, there exists a set of cycles $Y \subseteq \Omega_N[p]$ such that Y is conflict free, $P[Y] \subseteq S$ and ${}^{\bullet}p \subseteq T[Y]$.

Property 3.3 Every cycle in an augmented marked graph is marked.

Property 3.4 Every siphon in an augmented marked graph is marked.

Property 3.5 Let $(N, M_0; R)$ be an augmented marked graph. For every $r \in R$, there exists a minimal siphon which contains only one marked place r.

Property 3.6 For an augmented marked graph $(N, M_0; R)$, a R-siphon is covered by a set of cycles $Y \subseteq \Omega_N[R]$.

Property 3.7 Let S be a R-siphon of an augmented marked graph $(N, M_0; R)$. For every $t \in (S^{\bullet} \setminus {}^{\bullet}S)$, there does not exist any place $p \in (S \setminus R)$ such that $t \in p^{\bullet}$.

Property 3.8 For an augmented marked graph $(N, M_0; R)$, a NR-siphon contains itself as a marked trap.

Property 3.9 An augmented marked graph is live if and only if every minimal siphon would never become empty.

Property 3.10 A augmented marked graph is reversible if it it live.

Property 3.11 An augmented marked graph is live and reversible if and only if every minimal siphon would never become empty.

Property 3.12 An augmented marked graph is live and reversible if and only if every R-siphon would never become empty.

Property 3.13 An augmented marked graph is live and reversible if it satisfies the siphon-trap property.

Property 3.14 An augmented marked graph $(N, M_0; R)$ is live and reversible if every R-siphon contains a trap marked by M_0.

Property 3.15 For an augmented marked graph $(N, M_0; R)$, where $N = \langle P, T, F \rangle$, every place $p \in (P \setminus R)$ satisfies the cycle-inclusion property.

Property 3.16 Let $(N, M_0; R)$ an augmented marked graph. $(N, M_0; R)$ satisfies the siphon-trap property, or equivalently, every siphon contains a marked trap if and only if every place of R satisfies the cycle-inclusion property.

Property 3.17 An augmented marked graph $(N, M_0; R)$ is live and reversible if it satisfies the siphon-trap property, or equivalently, every place of R satisfies the cycle-inclusion property.

Property 3.18 Let $(N, M_0; R)$ be an augmented marked graph to be transformed into (N', M_0') as follows. For each place $r \in R$, where $D_r = \{ \langle t_{s1}, t_{h1} \rangle, \langle t_{s2}, t_{h2} \rangle, \ldots, \langle t_{skr}, t_{hkr} \rangle \}$, r is replaced by a set of places $Q = \{q_1, q_2, \ldots, q_{kr}\}$, such that $M_0'[p_i] = M_0[r]$ and $q_i^{\bullet} = \{t_{si}\}$ and $^{\bullet}q_i = \{t_{hi}\}$. Then, (N', M_0') is a marked graph.

Property 3.19 Let (N', M_0') be the R-transform of an augmented marked graph $(N, M_0; R)$. (N', M_0') is a live marked graph.

Property 3.20 Let $(N, M_0; R)$ be an augmented marked graph, and (N', M_0') be the R-transform of $(N, M_0; R)$, where a place $r \in R$ is replaced by a set of places $Q = \{q_1, q_2, \ldots, q_k\}$. Then, for each q_i in N', there exists a place invariant α_i of N' such that $\alpha_i[q_i] = 1$ and $\alpha_i[q] = 0$ for any $q \in (P_0 \setminus \{q_i\})$, where P_0 is the set of marked places in (N', M_0').

Property 3.21 Let $(N, M_0; R)$ be an augmented marked graph, where $R = \{r_1, r_2, \ldots, r_n\}$. Let (N', M_0') be the R-transform of $(N, M_0; R)$, where each r_i is replaced by a set of places Q_i, for $i = 1, 2, \ldots, n$. If every place in (N', M_0') belongs to a cycle, then there exists a place invariant α of N' such that $\alpha > 0$ and $\alpha[q_1] = \alpha[q_2] = \ldots = \alpha[q_k]$ for each $Q_i = \{q_1, q_2, \ldots, q_k\}$.

Property 3.22 Let $(N, M_0; R)$ be an augmented marked graph, and (N', M_0') be the R-transform of $(N, M_0; R)$. $(N, M_0; R)$ is bounded and conservative if and only if every place in (N', M_0') belongs to a cycle.

Chapter 4: Proper Augmented Marked Graphs

Property 4.1 A proper augmented marked graph $(N, M_0; R)$ is structurally a live, bounded and conservative marked graph if and only if, $\forall\, r \in R, |\,{}^{\bullet}r\,| = |\,r^{\bullet}\,| = 1$.

Property 4.2 A proper augmented marked graph $(N, M_0; R)$ is structurally an augmented marked graph unless $\forall\, r \in R, |\,{}^{\bullet}r\,| = |\,r^{\bullet}\,| = 1$.

Property 4.3 A proper augmented marked graph is bounded and conservative.

Property 4.4 Let $(N, M_0; R)$ be a proper augmented marked graph, and (N', M_0') be the R-transform of $(N, M_0; R)$. (N', M_0') is a marked graph which is live, bounded, conservative and strongly connected, or a set of disjoint marked graphs which are live, bounded, conservative and strongly connected.

Property 4.5 A proper augmented marked graph is T-coverable.

Property 4.6 Let $(N, M_0; R)$ be a proper augmented marked graph, and (N', M_0') be the R-transform of $(N, M_0; R)$. For any $\gamma \in \Omega_{N'}$, there exists $Y \subseteq \Omega_{N'}$, such that $\gamma \in Y$ and $T[Y] = {}^{\bullet}P[Y] \cup P[Y]^{\bullet}$.

Property 4.7 Let $(N, M_0; R)$ be a proper augmented marked graph. For any place p in $(N, M_0; R)$, there exists a set of cycles $Y \subseteq \Omega_N$, such that $p \in P[Y]$ and $T[Y] = {}^{\bullet}P[Y] \cup P[Y]^{\bullet}$.

Property 4.8 A proper augmented marked graph is P-coverable.

Property 4.9 A proper augmented marked graph is both P-coverable and T-coverable.

Chapter 5: Composition of Augmented Marked Graphs

Property 5.1 Let $(N_1, M_{10}; R_1)$ and $(N_2, M_{20}; R_2)$ be two augmented marked graphs. $R_1' = \{r_{11}, r_{12}, \ldots, r_{1k}\} \subseteq R_1$ and $R_2' = \{r_{21}, r_{22}, \ldots, r_{2k}\} \subseteq R_2$ are the common resource places, where $M_{10}(R_1') = M_{20}(R_2')$. Suppose that r_{11} and r_{21} are to be fused into one single place r_1, r_{12} and r_{22} into $r_2, \ldots, r_{1k}$ and r_{2k} into r_k. Then, the resulting PT-net so obtained is also an augmented marked graph $(N, M_0; R)$, where $R = (R_1 \setminus R_1') \cup (R_2 \setminus R_2') \cup \{r_1, r_2, \ldots, r_k\}$.

Property 5.2 The integrated augmented marked graph obtained by composing two proper augmented marked graphs via their common resource places is also a proper augmented marked graph.

Property 5.3 Let $(N, M_0; R)$ be the integrated augmented marked graph obtained by composing two augmented marked graphs $(N_1, M_{10}; R_1)$ and $(N_2, M_{20}; R_2)$ via a set of common resource places $\{(r_{11}, r_{21}), (r_{12}, r_{22}), \ldots, (r_{1k}, r_{2k})\}$, where $r_{11}, r_{12}, \ldots,$

$r_{1k} \in R_1$ and $r_{21}, r_{22}, \ldots, r_{2k} \in R_2$. $(N_1, M_{10}; R_1)$ and $(N_2, M_{20}; R_2)$ are live if $(N, M_0; R)$ is live.

Property 5.4 Let $(N, M_0; R)$ be the integrated augmented marked graph obtained by composing two augmented marked graphs $(N_1, M_{10}; R_1)$ and $(N_2, M_{20}; R_2)$ via a set of common resource places $\{(r_{11}, r_{21}), (r_{12}, r_{22}), \ldots, (r_{1k}, r_{2k})\}$ where $r_{11}, r_{12}, \ldots, r_{1k} \in R_1$, $r_{21}, r_{22}, \ldots, r_{2k} \in R_2$ and $M_{10}(r_{11}, r_{12}, \ldots, r_{1k}) = M_{20}(r_{21}, r_{22}, \ldots, r_{2k})$. $(N, M_0; R)$ is live and reversible if and only if $(N_1, M_{10}; R_1)$ and $(N_2, M_{20}; R_2)$ are live and no R_F-siphons in $(N, M_0; R)$ would eventually become empty.

Property 5.5 Let $(N_1, M_{10}; R_1)$ and $(N_2, M_{20}; R_2)$ be augmented marked graphs, where every place in R_1 and R_2 satisfies the cycle-inclusion property. Let $(N, M_0; R)$ be the integrated augmented marked graph obtained by composing $(N_1, M_{10}; R_1)$ and $(N_2, M_{20}; R_2)$ via their common resource places. $(N, M_0; R)$ is live and reversible if every place in R_F satisfies the cycle-inclusion property.

Property 5.6 Let $(N_1, M_{10}; R_1)$ and $(N_2, M_{20}; R_2)$ be augmented marked graphs, satisfying the siphon-trap property. Let $(N, M_0; R)$ be the integrated augmented marked graph obtained by composing $(N_1, M_{10}; R_1)$ and $(N_2, M_{20}; R_2)$ via their common resource places. $(N, M_0; R)$ is live and reversible if every place in R_F contains a marked trap.

Property 5.7 Let $(N, M_0; R)$ be the integrated augmented marked graph obtained by composing two augmented marked graphs $(N_1, M_{10}; R_1)$ and $(N_2, M_{20}; R_2)$ via a set of common resource places $\{(r_{11}, r_{21}), (r_{12}, r_{22}), \ldots, (r_{1k}, r_{2k})\}$ where $r_{11}, r_{12}, \ldots, r_{1k} \in R_1$, $r_{21}, r_{22}, \ldots, r_{2k} \in R_2$ and $M_{10}(r_{11}, r_{12}, \ldots, r_{1k}) = M_{20}(r_{21}, r_{22}, \ldots, r_{2k})$. $(N, M_0; R)$ is bounded if and only if $(N_1, M_{10}; R_1)$ and $(N_2, M_{20}; R_2)$ are bounded.

Property 5.8 Let $(N, M_0; R)$ be the integrated augmented marked graph obtained by composing two augmented marked graphs $(N_1, M_{10}; R_1)$ and $(N_2, M_{20}; R_2)$ via a set of common resource places $\{(r_{11}, r_{21}), (r_{12}, r_{22}), \ldots, (r_{1k}, r_{2k})\}$, where $r_{11}, r_{12}, \ldots, r_{1k} \in R_1$, $r_{21}, r_{22}, \ldots, r_{2k} \in R_2$ and $M_{10}(r_{11}, r_{12}, \ldots, r_{1k}) = M_{20}(r_{21}, r_{22}, \ldots, r_{2k})$. $(N, M_0; R)$ is conservative if and only if $(N_1, M_{10}; R_1)$ and $(N_2, M_{20}; R_2)$ are conservative.

Property 5.9 Let $(N, M_0; R)$ be the integrated augmented marked graph obtained by composing two augmented marked graphs $(N_1, M_{10}; R_1)$ and $(N_2, M_{20}; R_2)$ via a set of common resource places $\{(r_{11}, r_{21}), (r_{12}, r_{22}), \ldots, (r_{1k}, r_{2k})\}$, where $r_{11}, r_{12}, \ldots, r_{1k} \in R_1$, $r_{21}, r_{22}, \ldots, r_{2k} \in R_2$ and $M_{10}(r_{11}, r_{12}, \ldots, r_{1k}) = M_{20}(r_{21}, r_{22}, \ldots, r_{2k})$. $(N, M_0; R)$ is bounded and conservative if and only if $(N_1, M_{10}; R_1)$ and $(N_2, M_{20}; R_2)$ are bounded and conservative.

Property 5.10 Let $(N, M_0; R)$ be the integrated augmented marked graph obtained by composing two proper augmented marked graphs $(N_1, M_{10}; R_1)$ and $(N_2, M_{20}; R_2)$ via a set of common resource places $\{(r_{11}, r_{21}), (r_{12}, r_{22}), \ldots, (r_{1k}, r_{2k})\}$, where $r_{11}, r_{12}, \ldots, r_{1k} \in R_1$, $r_{21}, r_{22}, \ldots, r_{2k} \in R_2$ and $M_{10}(r_{11}, r_{12}, \ldots, r_{1k}) = M_{20}(r_{21}, r_{22}, \ldots, r_{2k})$. $(N, M_0; R)$ is bounded and conservative.

Appendix B: Algorithms for Checking the Properties of Augmented Marked Graphs

This appendix lists the algorithms for checking the properties of augmented marked graphs (Chap. 3), and the algorithms for checking the preservation of properties in the composition of augmented marked graphs (Chap. 5).

Chapter 3: Augmented Marked Graphs

Algorithms 3.1 and 3.2 check the liveness and reversibility of an augmented marked graph. Algorithm 3.1 is based on R-siphons, while Algorithm 3.2 is based on R-siphons and cycle-inclusion property. Algorithm 3.3 checks the boundedness and conservativeness of augmented marked graph, based on R-transform.

Algorithm 3.1 Checking the liveness and reversibility of an augmented marked graph $(N, M_0; R)$.

Step 1.   Find all R-siphons based on $\Omega_N[R]$.

Step 2.   Check if every R-siphon contains a marked trap. If yes, report $(N, M_0; R)$ is live and reversible. Otherwise, go to Step 3.

Step 3.   For each R-siphon which does not contain any marked trap, check if it would never become empty. If yes, report $(N, M_0; R)$ is live and reversible. Otherwise, report $(N, M_0; R)$ is neither live nor reversible.

Algorithm 3.2 Checking the liveness and reversibility of an augmented marked graph $(N, M_0; R)$.

Step 1.   Check if every $r \in R$ satisfies the cycle-inclusion property. If yes, report $(N, M_0; R)$ is live and reversible. Otherwise go to Step 2.

Step 2.   Let $R' \subseteq R$ be the set of places which do not satisfy the cycle-inclusion property. Based on $\Omega_N[R']$, find all R-siphons which contain at least one place in R'.

Step 3.   For each R-siphon identified in Step 2, check if it contains a marked trap. If yes, report $(N, M_0; R)$ is live and reversible. Otherwise, go to Step 4.

Step 4.   For each R-siphon identified in Step 2 that does not contain any marked trap, check if it would never become empty. If yes, report $(N, M_0; R)$ is live and reversible. Otherwise, report $(N, M_0; R)$ is neither live nor reversible.

Algorithm 3.3 Checking the boundedness and conservativeness of an augmented marked graph (N, M_0; R).

Step 1.   Create the R-transform (N′, M_0′) of (N, M_0; R).
Step 2.   Find the set of cycles $\Omega_{N'}$ in N′.
Step 3.   For each place p in (N′, M_0′), check if there exists a cycle $\gamma \in \Omega_{N'}$ such that p $\in$ P[γ]. If yes, report that (N, M_0; R) is bounded and conservative. Otherwise, report that (N, M_0; R) is neither bounded nor conservative.

Chapter 5: Composition of Augmented Marked Graphs

Algorithms 5.1 and 5.2 check the liveness and reversibility of the integrated augmented marked graphs obtained by composing two augmented marked graphs via their common resource places. Algorithm 5.1 is based on R_F-siphon, while Algorithm 5.2 is based on R_F-siphon and cycle-inclusion property.

Algorithm 5.1 Checking the liveness and reversibility of the integrated augmented marked graph (N, M_0; R), obtained by composing two augmented marked graphs (N_1, M_{10}; R_1) and (N_2, M_{20}; R_2).

Step 1.   Find all the R-siphons in (N_1, M_{10}; R_1) based on $\Omega_{N1}[R_1]$. Likewise, find all the R-siphons in (N_2, M_{20}; R_2) based on $\Omega_{N2}[R_2]$.
Step 2.   If all the R-siphons in (N_1, M_{10}; R_1) and (N_1, M_{10}; R_1) would never become empty, then proceed to Step 3. Otherwise, report that (N, M_0; R) is neither live nor reversible.
Step 3.   Find all the R_F-siphons in (N, M_0; R) based on $\Omega_N[R_F]$.
Step 4.   If all the R_F-siphons in (N, M_0; R) would never become empty, then report (N, M_0; R) is live nor reversible. Otherwise, report that (N, M_0; R) is neither live nor reversible.

Algorithm 5.2 Checking the liveness and reversibility of the integrated augmented marked graph (N, M_0; R), obtained by composing two augmented marked graphs (N_1, M_{10}; R_1) and (N_2, M_{20}; R_2).

Step 1.   For (N_1, M_{10}; R_1), check if the places in R_1 satisfy the cycle-inclusion property. Likewise, for (N_2, M_{20}; R_2), check if the places in R_2 satisfy the cycle-inclusion property.
Step 2.   Suppose the places in R_1 and R_2 satisfy the cycle-inclusion property. Then, for (N, M_0; R), check if the places in R_F satisfy the cycle-inclusion property.

Step 3.   If the places in R_F satisfy the cycle-inclusion property, report that $(N, M_0; R)$ is live and reversible. Otherwise, proceed to Step 4.

Step 4.   Find all the R-siphons in $(N_1, M_{10}; R_1)$ based on $\Omega_{N1}[R_1]$. Likewise, find all the R-siphons in $(N_2, M_{20}; R_2)$ based on $\Omega_{N2}[R_2]$.

Step 5.   If all the R-siphons in $(N_1, M_{10}; R_1)$ and $(N_1, M_{10}; R_1)$ would never become empty, then proceed to Step 6. Otherwise, report that $(N, M_0; R)$ is neither live nor reversible.

Step 6.   Find all the R_F-siphons in $(N, M_0; R)$ based on $\Omega_N[R_F]$.

Step 7.   If all the R_F-siphons in $(N, M_0; R)$ would never become empty, then report $(N, M_0; R)$ is live nor reversible. Otherwise, report that $(N, M_0; R)$ is neither live nor reversible.

Index